mediterraneo

350

mediterraneo

delicious recipes from the Mediterranean

Clare Ferguson
photography by Martin Brigdale

RYLAND
PETERS
& SMALL
LONDON NEW YORK

Dedication

To Ian Ferguson, my husband, who first took me to Greece all those years ago.

First published in the United States in 2004
by Ryland Peters & Small, Inc.
519 Broadway, 5th Floor
New York, NY 10012

www.rylandpeters.com

10 9 8 7 6 5 4 3 2

Library of Congress Cataloging-in-Publication Data

Ferguson, Clare.

Mediterraneo : delicious recipes from the Mediterranean / Clare Ferguson ; photography by Martin Brigdale.

p. cm.

ISBN 1-84172-570-6

1. Cookery, Mediterranean. I. Title.

TX725.M35F4723 2004

641.59'1822--dc22 2003017435

Printed and bound in China

Author's Acknowledgments

My thanks to Fiona Lindsay and Linda Shanks of Limelight Management. My gratitude to all those keen tasters who ventured opinions about the recipes or helped make decisions about the names of dishes, including Pada Rossin-Kelly, Marie-Pierre Moine, Maria-Jose Seville Swan, and Luis Peral Aranda. I am glad of all those who made Melianou in Zakynthos, Greece, such a splendid place to be.

Assistant Food Stylist: Pippa Cuthbert

Additional Researchers: Pippa Cuthbert, Ylva Powlett, Paola Rossin-Kelly, Maria-Jose Sevilla Swan, Elsa Petersen-Schepelern, Rena Salomon, Patricia and David Galloway, Marie-Pierre Moine Rosemary Barron, Luis Peral Aranda,

Word Processors: Liz Spicer, Pippa Cuthbert, Vicky Peterson

I am grateful for my favorite stallholders in the Portobello Road Market, London W11, for their exuberance, and to my valued Notting Hill food suppliers.

Though I am grateful for the advice, opinions, and skills of all those mentioned, any imperfections in these pages must be my responsibility, not theirs.

Publisher's Acknowledgments

Photograph on page 4 by Ian Wallace.

Senior Designer Steve Painter
Commissioning Editor Elsa Petersen-Schepelern
Editor Susan Stuck
Production Patricia Harrington
Art Director Gabriella Le Grazie
Publishing Director Alison Starling

Food Stylist Clare Ferguson
Prop Stylist Helen Trent
Indexer Hilary Bird

Notes

- All spoon measurements are level unless otherwise stated.
- All herbs are fresh, unless specified otherwise.
- Ingredients in this book are available from larger supermarkets, specialty food stores. See page 142 for mail order sources.
- For all recipes requiring dough or batter, liquid measurements are given as a guide. Always add liquid gradually to achieve the desired consistency, rather than adding it all at once. Use your eyes and your sense of touch to achieve the best results. If you don't use the flour specified in a recipe, the result may be affected.
- Eggs are large unless otherwise specified. Uncooked or partially cooked eggs should not be served to the very old, frail, young children, pregnant women, or those with compromised immune systems.
- Ovens should be preheated to the specified temperature. Recipes in this cookbook were tested using a convection oven. If using a conventional oven raise the oven temperature or follow the manufacturer's instructions.

contents

from the rock of gibraltar to the wine dark sea

My fascination with the Mediterranean was born when I first wandered through the violet shadows and dazzling sunlight of the canvas-covered Cours Saleya, the great food market in Nice. Now, three decades later, we visit our own *spitaiki* (little house) on a Greek island and make frequent trips to Spain, Italy, Cyprus, and Malta to continue to fuel the passion. The many facets of Mediterranean life continue to delight us. Good food is always a revelation, but Mediterranean food is vividly sensual: full of flavor and dazzling freshness. It is distinctive, subtle, racy, and intriguing.

Bordering the shores of the northern Mediterranean are Spain, southern France, Italy, Greece, and their islands, home of many of the world's best-loved dishes. All have endured endless invasions and conquests, from outside the area, and from each other, providing lively colonization and cultural cross-fertilization that shows in their food.

Sardinia, for example, was conquered first, by Carthage, then Rome. Arabs made their contribution, then Spain, resident over four centuries, left behind Catalan foods such as saffron, empanadas, and rich meat stews. Italian influences continued with the rule of Pisa and Genoa in the 1200s, then later French contributions flourished under the Duke of Savoy. The history of this one small island is typical of the cultural exchanges that occurred throughout the region, but also explains some of the paradoxical diversity: why Sardinia, Sicily, Campania, and Tuscany, for example, show such differing food styles yet rich similarities in food traditions and hospitality.

Greece's *mezethes* (communal snacks) echo Ottoman and Middle Eastern tradition. However, the similar Spanish tapas came about because the bread slices used as "lids" (or *tapas*) on top of glasses of wine developed into delicious bar nibbles.

Since wheat, olives, and grapes have long underpinned Mediterranean food cultures, bread, olive oil, and wine are basic essentials. A wealth of fresh seasonal fruits and vegetables, including the beloved tomato, herbs, and garlic, are constants. Seafood holds a special place, thanks to the Catholic traditions of Lenten fasts, which avoided meat, and the formerly strict rule that fish must be eaten on Friday. Even the wealth of local fresh fish wasn't enough—Scandinavian cod was salted and dried to help to fulfil the demand; exported as *morue* to Provence, stockfish to Italy, and *bacalao* to Spain.

Though it is easy to appreciate the romance of the Mediterranean, it is the tumultuous accidents of history, politics, and geography, the extremes of climate, terrain, and local tradition, along with the often capricious harvest of land and sea, that make this cuisine so interesting. It is generous yet frugal; poetic but practical; pleasurable but also remarkably healthy.

It is the outdoor markets which encapsulate the quality and verve of Mediterranean food and cooking. Peaches and grapes still covered with bloom rest beside pyramids of artichokes and tomatoes. Strings of garlic hang next to garlands of *saucissons*. On the next stall, red mullet contrast with silver anchovies, and striped clams blow bubbles beside trays of live blue crabs. Salad leaves in baskets display every size, tone, and texture imaginable. Pungent green herbs have fragrant appeal. Cheeses, loaves, and flatbreads are piled on stall after stall. Wild mushrooms, chestnuts, and plums tumble from boxes, and everywhere there are rainbow arrays of olives, their oil and local wines. Superb, authentic food, honestly produced, in its natural season is always heaven.

Envisage sunlit piazzas, flowering citrus trees, fountains and happy crowds eating gelati. Imagine little Greek harborside *kafenions* with rickety chairs, octopus hung up to dry, and boats bobbing nearby. Elsewhere, under the plane trees or gnarled olive trees, there are extended families, aged from 8 days to 8 decades old, reveling in exuberant celebration meals. Imagine a terraced hillside in Provence with a bistro serving robust local wines straight from the barrel, with local goat cheese and crusty bread.

Ideal to cook at home on busy weekdays or at weekends when celebrations are called for – the ideas in this book give just a taste of the flavors, versatility, and beauty of these great cuisines.

escabech
100g
45.00F

appetizers

Mediterranean appetizers are often small, intensely flavored, colorful, but relaxed. People rarely drink without eating: small snacks are served automatically in most taverns, requested or not—a good practice.

Italian antipasti are designed to be intriguing, to promote camaraderie, show hospitality, and echo the season and region.

Spanish tapas, from *tapar* meaning "to cover," refers to slices of bread, originally used to cover sherry glasses in the hot, insect-ridden bars of Andalucia. The word has come to mean tiny, delicious bar snacks of all kinds.

In eastern tradition, many small portions of savory foods were set out on low tables. People shared, fed each other, and relaxed with cool drinks, the origin of today's Greek and Turkish meze.

In Provence, hors d'oeuvres, often cold, small but piquant, eaten al fresco with an anise aperitif or a local wine, are considered the beginning of the meal proper.

Whatever appetite-arousers you choose, remember, as Mediterraneans do, to keep them light, colorful, and small.

tigre tapas

Versions of this delicious Spanish snack, also known as *mejillones en gabardina* (mussels in overcoats), can be found everywhere from Istanbul to Sicily, from Provence to Morocco—but in Spain mussels are particularly succulent, plump, and colorful. Cook mussels in their shells for the minimum time, just until they open and the flesh sets. Make a frothy batter, use it to coat and cook the mussels a second time, then serve however you prefer. As bar snacks or tapas, these are good nibbled straight from the shell, but skewers also look pretty and are practical to serve. Delicious with chilled fino sherry, white wine, dry cava, or beer.

1 lb. large, live mussels, in the shell

1 onion, sliced

2 fresh bay leaves, bruised

⅔ cup hot stock, white wine, or fino sherry

virgin olive oil or peanut oil, for deep-frying

batter

⅔ cup all-purpose flour

1 teaspoon hot oak-smoked Spanish paprika

½ teaspoon freshly ground black pepper

a pinch of saffron threads,
or 2 envelopes powdered saffron

½ teaspoon coarse salt

2 extra-large eggs, separated

an electric deep-fryer or deep skillet

toothpicks (optional)

serves 4

Scrub the mussels and discard any "beards" or threads. Tap them all gently against the work surface and discard any that don't close. If any feel very heavy, discard them also, because they're probably filled with sand.

Put the mussels, onion, bay leaves, and stock in a large saucepan and cover. Bring to a boil and cook hard for 2–3 minutes or until the shells open.

Remove the cooked mussels, discard any that haven't opened and remove and discard the empty top shells. Retain the mussels on the half-shell (or shell them all if you like). Boil the cooking liquid for several minutes to intensify the flavor, then pour through a strainer. Reserve ½ cup of the cooking liquid.

Fill a deep skillet one-third full with the oil, or an electric deep-fryer to the manufacturer's recommended level. Heat to 375°F or until a ½-inch cube of bread browns in 30 seconds.

To make the batter, sift the flour, paprika, and black pepper into a bowl. If using saffron threads, grind them finely with the salt using a mortar and pestle or the blade of a knife. Add to the dry ingredients.

Put the egg whites in another bowl and beat until soft peaks form. Set aside.

Add the reserved mussel liquid and egg yolks to the flour and beat to make a soft batter. Fold in the egg whites.

Dip the mussels, still on their half-shells (or shelled mussels threaded in threes onto toothpicks) into the batter. Add to the hot oil, in batches of 5–6. Cook for 2–2½ minutes or until golden, crisp, and fragrant. Serve piled on small serving dishes, as a snack or appetizer.

squid with mayonnaise
sepia con alioli

⅔–1⅓ cups semolina flour

½–1 teaspoon sea salt

½–1 teaspoon dried oregano or marjoram leaves, crumbled

8 medium squid tubes, sliced into ½-inch rounds

2 cups virgin olive oil, for deep-frying

alioli

6–8 fat garlic cloves, crushed

½ teaspoon sea salt

½ cup extra virgin olive oil

2 lemons, halved (optional)

freshly ground black pepper

an electric deep-fryer

serves 4

Cuttlefish or squid, either whole tiny ones or larger ones sliced into rings, are favorites all round the Mediterranean, and in good bars and restaurants worldwide. In Spain, they are floured and sizzled until crisp, often accompanied by a stinging, garlicky mayonnaise. Traditional Spanish alioli contains salt, garlic, and olive oil and is a thick, dense, sticky emulsion. Most recipes these days—modified for ease and speed but not necessarily for accuracy—include an egg yolk like the Provençal aïoli; some made in a food processor may even require a whole egg. Remember that powerful flavors are the norm in such a dish.

Put the semolina flour, salt, and oregano in a bowl. Pat the squid rings dry with paper towels and toss them in the flour mixture until well coated. Set them aside, not touching, while you make the sauce.

To make the alioli, crush the garlic and salt to a sticky paste with a mortar and pestle. Pour in the oil in a fine stream, beating constantly in one direction until creamy. Continue adding and mixing to form a thick, glossy emulsion. Alternatively, use a bowl and a hand-held electric mixer.

Meanwhile, fill a deep-fryer to the manufacturer's recommended level and heat to 375°F. Fry the prepared squid or cuttlefish in the hot oil in batches of about 8. Cook for 30–45 seconds, the minimum time it takes to set the seafood to firm whiteness and make the coating crisp. Remove, drain, and keep hot. Continue until all are cooked.

Serve a pile of squid rings on each plate, with ½ lemon, if using, and a large spoonful of the garlicky dipping sauce beside or in bowls.

Variation Provençal aïoli, another version of alioli, can be made in a food processor, but the quantities must be larger to let the blades run. Put the garlic and salt from the main recipe in a food processor, plus 2 egg yolks and 1 whole egg and blend until creamy. Gradually pour in about ¾ cup olive oil until the mixture is thick and emulsified. You will find it becomes very thick. Blend in 1–2 tablespoons of lemon juice at the end. Serves 8 (more than the main recipe). If serving later, cover closely with plastic wrap and keep in the refrigerator for up to 3 days.

These tiny balls of ground fish, with bread, herbs, and typically Italian seasonings, are pan-fried then served with a deglazed pan sauce as an antipasto. The Spanish version is called *albóndigas*, usually served dry, without a sauce. It is popular as a bar snack, part of a tapas selection. Although swordfish is particularly delicious, you could substitute tuna, halibut, porgy, or other dense-fleshed fish. Serve with chilled white wine such as pinot grigio or sauvignon blanc.

italian swordfish balls
polpette di pesce spada

12 oz. swordfish, skinned, boned, and cut into cubes

2 cups crumbled stale bread

1 onion, coarsely grated

¼ cup capers, drained and chopped

1 tablespoon drained and chopped pickled gherkins (cornichons)

freshly squeezed juice of 1 lemon

1 teaspoon freshly ground white pepper

8 canned anchovies, drained and mashed to a pulp

⅓ cup extra virgin olive oil

2 tablespoons pine nuts

freshly grated zest and juice of 1 unwaxed orange

a large handful of fresh flat-leaf parsley, chopped

bread, to serve

serves 4–6

Put the fish, bread, onion, capers, gherkins, lemon juice, pepper, and half the anchovies in a food processor. Pulse in brief bursts to a soft, dense paste, but don't over-process. Transfer to a work surface and take heaping teaspoons of the mixture, squeeze them to make firm, then roll each portion into a neat ball. You should have 36, about 1 inch diameter.

Put half the oil in a skillet, preferably nonstick, and heat until very hot. Add half the fish balls, and shake the pan over medium-high heat for 3–4 minutes, so the balls roll and turn and brown all over. Test one: it should feel dense and firm and be the same color right through. Remove the balls from the pan and keep hot on a plate. Add the remaining oil to the pan and cook the remaining balls in the same way.

Reserve ¼ cup of the oil in the pan and discard the remainder. Return the reserved oil to the pan, add the pine nuts and shake and stir until golden brown, then remove with a slotted spoon. Keep hot with the fish balls.

Add the orange zest and juice and remaining anchovies to the pan. Stir over medium heat until syrupy. Add half the parsley and extra lemon juice, if necessary.

Serve the fish balls hot, warm or cool with the sauce. Sprinkle with the remaining parsley and serve with crusty bread or a crisp Italian flatbread.

spanish clams with ham

almejas con jamón

2 tablespoons extra virgin olive oil

1 lb. small live clams in the shell, such as littlenecks

2 oz. jamón serrano or prosciutto, cut into thin strips

1 small green chile, seeded and chopped

2 garlic cloves, sliced

¼ cup white wine or cider

2 tablespoons chopped scallion tops, chives, or parsley

serves 4

Mediterranean live clams usually go straight into the cooking pot, with oil and garlic. Herbs and a splash of wine are sometimes added. However, because Spanish cured hams are so exceptional, adding even a little seasons and enlivens many such savory dishes. *Mar i montaña* (sea and mountains) is a typically Catalan cooking idea which has spread worldwide. Catalans also revel in extraordinary seasonings, aromatic herbs, chocolate, juniper, cinnamon with game, and saffron in both sweet and savory dishes. A revelation.

Put the olive oil, clams, ham, chile, and garlic in a flameproof casserole and stir over high heat. When the ham is cooked and the clams begin to open, add the wine, cover the pan, and tilt it several times to mix the ingredients. Cook on high for a further 2–3 minutes or until all clams have opened and are cooked.

Sprinkle with chopped scallions. Cover again for 1 minute, then ladle into shallow soup bowls.

Barcelona, Seville, and Madrid buzz with culinary finesse, and today's young chefs often incorporate outside influences, with great skill, into classic dishes. Although raw tuna with soy sauce in its marinade seems more like a Japanese idea than a Spanish one, it is a well-loved, new-style seafood tapas dish. Select a neat rectangle of premium-quality tuna—at least 1 inch thick and skinless, boneless, and well trimmed of all cartilage. Have small forks or wooden toothpicks for spearing each mouthful, and serve with a chilled sparkling wine such as cava or a chilled fino sherry.

spanish marinated tuna
bonito marinado

8 oz. sushi-grade fresh tuna, such as loin of yellowfin, cut into ½-inch chunks

1 tablespoon light soy sauce

1 tablespoon sherry vinegar

1 teaspoon toasted sesame oil

1 tablespoon extra virgin olive oil

1 garlic clove, crushed

1 tablespoon toasted sesame seeds (optional)

1 tablespoon blue poppy seeds (optional)

crisp salad leaves or green herbs (optional)

serves 4

Put the tuna, soy sauce, vinegar, sesame oil, olive oil, and garlic in a bowl and stir well. Cover and let marinate in the refrigerator for 5 minutes or up to 2 hours.

Drain, then arrange the cubes, in rows, on small serving dishes. Add lines of the sesame and poppy seeds, if using, then sprinkle with the marinade or leave plain. Add a few salad leaves, if using. Serve the remaining marinade in 4 tiny dipping bowls.

In the south of France, there are superb dishes made using "blue shells," as the French often call mussels. Sometimes, on the Atlantic seaboard of France, they are cooked at the beach under a layer of pine needles—an ancient technique. In other parts of the country, they may be poached with rice—with or without spices—then filled with the rice and made into small packages. Use one shell to scrape out the mussel and its filling from the other shell. If you decide to tie the packages, you will need two yards of raffia or coarse twine. Drink with chilled Pernod and ice water or with a robust Minervois or Languedoc wine.

french stuffed mussels
moules farcies

1 lb. fresh live mussels, in the shell

⅓ cup chopped fresh flat-leaf parsley

1 small head of fennel, sliced

4 garlic cloves, chopped

2 tablespoons extra virgin olive oil

1 cup medium-dry white wine

¾ cup boiling fish stock or boiling water

1 cup long-grain white rice

2 teaspoons ground cinnamon or
1 cinnamon stick, bruised

1 dried red chile, seeded

1 cup finely chopped or grated Gruyère cheese (optional)

raffia or twine, cut into 8-inch lengths

a baking sheet

serves 4

Scrub the mussels and discard any "beards" or threads. Tap them all gently against the work surface and discard any that don't close. If any feel very heavy, discard them also, because they're probably filled with sand.

Put the mussels, parsley, fennel, garlic, olive oil, and white wine in a large saucepan. Bring to a boil (about 3–4 minutes), cover the pan, and cook for 2 minutes or until some of the mussels have opened. Remove these, cover, and continue cooking until all are done. Remove them all from the pan and keep in a bowl. Remove and discard any that haven't opened. Return the cooking liquid to the pan.

Add the boiling stock, rice, cinnamon, and chile to the saucepan and return to a boil. Reduce the heat to very low and cover the pan. Cook for 8 minutes, then push the reserved mussels down deep into the rice to reheat.

Remove the mussels, pushing the cooked rice into each pair of shells to fill them. Tie into a package with the raffia. Serve hot. Alternatively, set the stuffed mussels on a baking tray and sprinkle with cheese. Broil for 3–4 minutes until sizzling and hot. Eat with your fingers or a small fork.

Piquillo peppers are vividly red, mildly spicy-hot, often sold roasted and peeled in cans or jars. The classic Spanish dish of spicy piquillos, stuffed with creamy salt cod or with cheese, then batter-covered and fried, is certainly superb, but this lighter version makes great easy snack food and can be ready in under 10 minutes. Buy piquillo peppers from Hispanic stores and good gourmet stores or use similar sweet peppers in cans or jars. Serve with a chilled fino or amontillado sherry, crusty bread and baby salad greens.

spanish stuffed peppers

piquillos rellenos

6 oz. canned peeled sweet peppers or pimientos, such as piquillos

¼ cup olive oil

3–4 garlic cloves, chopped

2 cups canned white beans (15 oz. can), such as cannellini or lima beans, partially drained (reserve the liquid)

2 tablespoons sherry vinegar

a handful of fresh thyme or mint, chopped

a handful of baby salad greens such as spinach, watercress, or flat-leaf parsley

sea salt and freshly ground black pepper

serves 4

Drain the peppers, reserving the liquid. Pat dry with paper towels.

Heat the oil, garlic, and part-drained white beans in a nonstick skillet and mash with a fork to a thick, coarse paste. Add 1 tablespoon of the sherry vinegar and 1 tablespoon of bean liquid, stir, then season well with salt and pepper. Let cool slightly, then stuff each pepper with the mixture and sprinkle with the thyme.

Cut each piquillo into thick slices or leave whole. Serve on 4 plates, adding some greens to each. Trickle a tablespoon of the preserving liquid and a few drops of vinegar (if available) before serving.

Variation Instead of canned peppers, use 4 sweet red peppers, halved lengthwise and seeded. Grill them skin side up until blistered. Rub off the skins, stuff with the mixture, roll up, then serve as in the main recipe.

This tapas-type dish is sometimes found in bars in Barcelona and elsewhere in Spain served the local rosé or red wine, well chilled: a delicious combination. If you can't find Spanish Cabrales cheese, use a mature Cheddar.

eggplant cheese fritters
berenjenas con queso

1 large eggplant, about 12 oz.

6–7 oz. strong, meltable cheese such as Cabrales or mature Cheddar

⅔ cup all-purpose flour, seasoned with salt and pepper

2 eggs, well beaten with a fork

about 2 cups virgin olive oil or safflower oil, for frying

salsa

2 medium vine-ripened tomatoes, chopped

¼ cup chile oil, or olive oil mixed with ½ teaspoon Tabasco sauce

4 teaspoons red wine vinegar or sherry vinegar

12 fresh basil leaves

sea salt and freshly ground black pepper

toothpicks

an electric deep-fryer

serves 4

Using a sharp, serrated knife, cut the eggplant crosswise into 18–24 thin slices about ¼ inch thick. Slice the cheese into pieces of the same thickness. Cut and piece them together to fit, sandwiching a slice of cheese between 2 slices of eggplant. To keep the "sandwiches" closed during cooking, push a wooden toothpick, at an angle, through each one.

Put the flour on a plate. Pour the beaten eggs into a shallow dish. Dip the eggplant "sandwiches" first into the flour, then into the beaten eggs, then in flour again to coat well all over.

Fill a deep skillet one-third full with the oil, or an electric fryer to the manufacturer's recommended level. Heat to 375°F or until a ½-inch cube of bread browns in 30 seconds. Slide some of the prepared "sandwiches" into the hot oil in batches of 3 and fry for 2–3 minutes on the first side. Using tongs, turn and cook for 1–2 minutes on the other side or until golden and crisp, with the cheese melting inside. Drain on crumpled paper towels while you coat and cook the rest.

Meanwhile, to make the salsa, put the tomatoes, chile oil, vinegar, basil leaves, salt, and pepper in a food processor. Pulse in brief bursts to a coarse mixture.

Serve the fritters hot with a trickle of the salsa, or with a little pot of salsa as a dip at the side of the plate.

Although often served towards the end of a Greek meal (like an English cheese savory used to be), this dish may also be served as an appetizer, part of a meze (literally, a "tableful"). Unlike the Cypriot version, which uses local haloumi cheese, the traditional *saganaki* uses strongly flavored, hard, dry, seasonal cheese such as kefalotyri. If unavailable, use mature Cheddar instead. Traditionally this is served in small, two-handled skillets brought, sizzling, to the table. The cheese is eaten with a fork or scooped onto crusty bread. Use best-quality olive oil: its taste makes a considerable difference.

sautéed greek cheese
saganaki

4 slices kefalotyri cheese or mature Cheddar, cut ¼-inch thick

all-purpose flour, for dusting

cold-pressed extra virgin olive oil, for cooking (preferably Greek)

coarsely ground black pepper

lemon wedges, to serve

serves 4

Dust each slice of cheese generously with flour, patting it all over. Heat 2 teaspoons of olive oil for each cheese piece (cook them singly or in pairs, depending on the size of the pan) in a small skillet until very hot. Using tongs, add 1–2 slices of floured cheese. Sauté for 1–1½ minutes or until golden, crusty, and aromatic and starting to soften inside.

Using a narrow spatula, carefully turn each piece over. Sauté for a further 45 seconds on the second side until crusty.

Serve directly from the dish, adding black pepper and a wedge of lemon, or slide onto a small plate. Continue until all the cheese is cooked. Eat while still hot, crusty, fragrant, and starting to melt.

Asparagus in season is pure delight and, whether it is the fine wild variety or the large cultivated type, it is considered a particular treat in Europe. Add the delicate sweetness of Parma ham, dried to crispness, and you have an unusual combination. Use white asparagus if you can find it (French and Italian greengrocers often stock this during early summer), though green asparagus is more usual. Serve with frizzante, such as Lambrusco, or a crisp, dry, white wine.

asparagus with prosciutto
asparagi con prosciutto

8 thin slices prosciutto, such as Parma ham, San Danièle, or jamón serrano, 6–7 oz.

1 lb. bunch of thick asparagus

2 tablespoons extra virgin olive oil or lemon-infused olive oil

a shallow baking tray

serves 4

Before turning on the oven, hang the slices of prosciutto over the grids of the top oven rack. Slide the rack into the oven, then turn it on to 300°F. Leave for 20 minutes or until the ham has dried and become crisp. Remove it carefully and set aside.

Using a vegetable peeler, peel 3 inches of the tough skin off the end of each asparagus spear, then snap off and discard any tough ends. Arrange the asparagus in a shallow baking tray and sprinkle with the oil. Cook under a preheated broiler for 6–8 minutes, or until the asparagus is wrinkled and tender.

Serve the asparagus with some of the hot oil from the broiler pan and some prosciutto "crisps," 2 for each person.

Gazpacho, the famous iced tomato soup from Andalucia—almost a liquid salad—is even better made with sweetly mellow Pedro Ximenez vinegar, found in Hispanic grocers or good wine merchants. This vinegar is produced from one of Spain's greatest wines. Serve the chilled soup in stemmed glasses, on a napkin sitting on a small plate, as seen in tapas bars and bodegas from Seville to Salvador. The quality of the tomatoes is important: choose well-flavored ones. Green bell peppers, always included in Andalucia, are not everyone's favorite, so omit it if you prefer.

gazpacho pedro ximenez

2 vine-ripened tomatoes, blanched, peeled, and finely chopped

½ red or white onion, finely chopped

1 cucumber, peeled and finely chopped

1 green bell pepper, halved, seeded, cored, and chopped

1 tablespoon tomato paste

2 garlic cloves, chopped

1 cup stale bread cubes, about 1 slice

3 tablespoons Pedro Ximenez vinegar, or sherry vinegar plus 1 tablespoon sweet sherry

1 tablespoon extra virgin olive oil

sea salt and freshly ground black pepper

green olive ice cubes

12 green Spanish olives, stuffed with anchovies or almonds

chilled sparkling water

serves 4–6

To make decorative ice cubes, start the day before. Set 12 stuffed olives in an ice cube tray. Fill it with sparkling water and freeze. Keep until serving time.

Put the tomatoes, onion, cucumber, pepper, if using, and the tomato paste in a food processor or blender. Add the garlic, stale bread, half the vinegar, all the oil, and 1¾ cups water. Purée the soup continuously until it becomes a smooth, brick-red mixture. Add salt and pepper to taste, then add the remaining vinegar. Blend again.

Pour into 4–6 stemmed glasses, each with 2–3 olive ice cubes. Set the remaining olives on the plate. Drink the soup straight from the glass: the olives act as additional seasoning.

Variations

- If you prefer, omit the olive-filled ice cubes and simply serve plain ice, with extra olives on the side.

- To make croutons, cut an additional 1–1½ slices of stale bread into ½ -inch cubes and sauté in extra virgin olive oil until crisp. Serve with the soup for sprinkling on top.

Chorizo, a paprika-rich, spicy, smoky, garlicky and sometimes piquant Spanish sausage, can be bought in links or in long, curved shapes, raw or cooked. It varies, depending on its area of production and the uses for which it is intended. Some types, larger and sold cooked and ready-sliced like salami, are also available as snack foods. This recipe needs the raw, spicy, link-type chorizo meant for cooking. Find it in specialist gourmet stores or Hispanic grocers.

chorizo in red wine

chorizo al rioja

1½ lb. uncooked chorizo sausage, or other dense, garlic-flavored pork sausage

2 tablespoons extra virgin olive oil

⅔ cup red Rioja wine

4 sprigs of thyme (optional)

freshly ground black pepper

torn bread, for dipping

serves 4

Cut the chorizo into ½-inch chunks. Heat half the oil in a large, nonstick skillet until very hot. Add half the chorizo and sauté on both sides for 1 minute each. Remove with a slotted spoon and keep hot. Add the remaining oil and remaining chorizo. Cook and remove as before.

Add the wine and thyme, if using, to the pan and swirl to dissolve the sediment. Cook gently to thicken and reduce the sauce. Pour the sauce over the hot chorizo and serve sprinkled with pepper, plus chunks of torn bread for dipping.

Note If chorizo is difficult to find, use cooked, garlicky kielbasa and add 2 teaspoons of paprika to the juices in the pan.

Spain's celebrated thick tortilla omelet is one of the world's most accommodating dishes: good for any occasion and particularly useful as a portable picnic food, a quick lunch dish eaten between slices of bread, or even a breakfast snack. Served with this scarlet sweet pepper sauce, it is delicious. Though I like it made with garlic, this is not a usual addition, so please yourself.

spanish potato omelet

tortilla de patata

½ cup extra virgin olive oil

2 lb. boiling potatoes, peeled and cut into 1-inch cubes

1 onion, sliced into rings

4 garlic cloves, finely chopped (optional)

6 eggs, beaten

¼ cup chopped flat-leaf parsley or scallion tops

sea salt and freshly ground black pepper

piquillo sauce

8 oz. can or jar of roasted sweet peppers, such as piquillos or pimientos

3 tablespoons sherry vinegar

serves 4–6

Heat the oil in a medium skillet, add the potatoes and onion, and cook over low heat for 12–14 minutes or until tender but not browned, moving them about with a spatula so that they cook evenly. Add the garlic, if using, for the last 2 minutes.

Put the eggs, salt, and pepper in a bowl and beat well.

Using a slotted spoon, remove the cooked potatoes and garlic from the pan and stir it into the egg mixture. Stir in the chopped parsley.

Quickly pour the egg mixture back into the hot skillet. Cook, not stirring, over low to moderate heat for 4–5 minutes or until firm, but do not let it brown too much. The top will still be wobbly, only part-cooked.

Holding a heatproof plate over the top of the omelet, quickly invert the pan, omelet, and plate. Slide the hot omelet back, upside down, to brown the other side for 2–3 minutes more, then remove from the pan and let cool for 5 minutes.

To make the sauce, put the sweet peppers, ⅓ cup of the liquid from the can (make it up with water if necessary) and the sherry vinegar in a blender. Purée to form a smooth, scarlet sauce.

Cut the omelet into chunks, segments, or cubes. Serve the sauce separately, spooning some over the pieces of tortilla.

Note In many Spanish bars and cafés, sliced zucchini, spinach, onion, or red bell peppers may be added to the potatoes for variety, flavor, and color, but plain potato is the most common and well loved at home and abroad.

In many parts of France, Italy and Spain, slices of bread are toasted over an open fire or on a stove-top grill pan. Garlic is rubbed roughly over the surface then top-quality olive oil trickled over the top, followed by a sprinkle of coarse salt. Simple and perfect. Delicious variations include crushed fresh tomato or a strongly flavored salty topping. Both versions are superb, but depend on smokiness, good bread, and pungent aromatics. Remember, a toaster will not do! This recipe is a variation on these simple themes

anchovy croutes with onions

croûtes d'anchois et oignons

1 medium baguette, cut into 8 diagonal slices

4 garlic cloves, unpeeled but coarsely crushed

2 tablespoons cold-pressed extra virgin olive oil

1 red onion, very finely sliced

2 large plum tomatoes, cut into ¼-inch pieces

12 marinated anchovies, halved lengthwise into strips

freshly ground black pepper

serves 4

Preheat a broiler, outdoor grill, or stove-top grill pan and cook 4 slices of bread briefly on one side only until crisp. While still hot, rub one crushed garlic clove all over both sides of toast until fragrant.

Repeat with the remaining bread and garlic. Trickle the olive oil over the top.

Using the blade of a knife as a guide, make diagonal lines of onion, tomatoes, and anchovies over each slice of toast. Sprinkle with pepper and serve while still warm and fragrant.

The Spanish are enthusiastic about peas and beans, fresh or dried. Little earthenware bowls of this warm salad are seen in tapas bars all over Spain. It is satisfying and good, especially when mopped up with a chunk of crusty bread and served with a robust red wine or chilled lager. Although Spanish cooks would usually soak the dried chickpeas, then cook them with a little bit of pork, this chorizo version is easy and particularly delicious. Sometimes *morcilla* (black pudding) or *butifarra* (white sausage) is used instead.

catalan chickpea salad
ensalada catalana de garbanzos

3 tablespoons extra virgin olive oil

1 red onion, sliced

2 garlic cloves, chopped

8 oz. cooking chorizo or other garlicky spiced pork sausage, sliced

2 bay leaves, bruised

2 tablespoons pine nuts, toasted in a dry skillet

2 cups canned chickpeas (15 oz. can), drained, with 2 tablespoons of their liquid

coarsely ground black pepper

1 small tomato, finely chopped

serves 4

Heat the oil in a skillet, add the onion, garlic, chorizo, and bay leaves and sauté over gentle heat for 5 minutes or until softened but not browned. Stir in the pine nuts and chickpeas with a little of their liquid. Heat through until the flavors are combined, mashing a little with a fork.

Sprinkle with pepper and tomato and serve hot, warm, or cool, but never chilled.

This intensely flavored French black olive paste, famous for centuries, is so named because one of its components, *tapena* (capers), contribute strongly to its essential flavors. It may also be called *la fachoira* or *"caviar" Niçois* in Nice. As well as salt-cured or dry-cured black olives, the other ingredients are garlic, anchovies, black pepper, oregano, and thyme (or basil for *fachoira*). Once, in St Remy de Provence, I tasted it with a dash of Cognac: it was superb. Extra virgin olive oil is essential.

tapenade

1 lb. dry or salt-cured, fleshy black olives, preferably Provençal

4 garlic cloves, peeled and crushed

8 canned anchovies, chopped

¼ cup capers (not rinsed)

1 teaspoon coarsely ground black pepper

¼ cup cold-pressed extra virgin olive oil

1 teaspoon fresh oregano, thyme, or basil

2 tablespoons Cognac (optional)

sea salt and freshly ground black pepper (optional)

to serve

your choice of:
hot toasted bread
baby vegetables
hard-cooked eggs

serves 8

Pit the olives and chop them finely. Using a mortar and pestle (the traditional way), crush the olives, then mash in the garlic, anchovies, capers, and pepper. Pound to a coarse paste. If using a food processor, use the pulse button in 5-second bursts to form a coarse paste. Trickle in the oil quickly, while pounding or pulsing, to create a creamy mash.

Stir in the oregano and Cognac, if using, at the end. Taste and season more, if needed. Serve cool with hot toast, baby vegetables, hard-cooked eggs, or a mixture.

Refrigerated and well covered, tapenade will keep for 2 weeks.

Variations

- Lemon juice can be used instead of the Cognac.

- Green olives can be used to make a green tapenade: sharper and less rich, but interesting, if untraditional.

All around the Mediterranean, fresh and dried peas, beans, and lentils are used in dips and spreads, as sauces with pasta, and in soups. Depending on the region and local herbs, different flavors and ingredients are used. Near Nice, Swiss chard stems and parsley may be added; in Italy, rosemary is used rather than oregano; and in North African immigrant communities, mint may be an option. The constant is dried fava beans, known as faba beans. The best are the skinless type: they cook quickly, taste better, and have a more delicate texture. Soak them for 4 hours or overnight in cold water, or cheat by putting them in a saucepan, covering them with boiling water, bringing to a boil, and soaking for 2 hours with the heat turned off. Drain, cover with cold water, bring to a boil, and simmer until tender. Drain again, season, and use as a dip or spread (or dilute as a sauce or soup).

italian bean dip

puré di fave

2 cups dried peeled fava beans

1 fresh bouquet garni of parsley, celery, bay leaf, and thyme

1 large onion, chopped

1 potato, unpeeled

4 garlic cloves, chopped

¼ cup first-pressed extra virgin olive oil, plus extra to serve (optional)

freshly squeezed juice of 1 lemon (4–5 tablespoons)

6 sprigs of oregano, chopped

sea salt and freshly ground black pepper

to serve

your choice of:
baby leafy vegetables
radishes
cucumber
crusty bread

serves 4

Soak and drain the beans as described above, then put them in a large saucepan with the bunch of herbs, onion, and potato and add 2 quarts boiling water. Bring to a boil, boil hard for 10 minutes, reduce the heat, and cook, partially covered, for 1½–2 hours or until you can crush the beans easily with your thumbnail.

Drain the vegetables, reserving 2–3 tablespoons of liquid. Discard the herbs. Working in batches if necessary, put the beans, potato, raw onion, and garlic in a food processor, with the olive oil, lemon juice, oregano, salt, and pepper. Blend in short bursts to a grainy but creamy purée.

Serve hot (as a side dish), warm, or cool, sprinkled with extra olive oil. Serve as a dip or spread with baby leafy vegetables, radishes, and cucumber or with bread chunks, or a combination.

Campo

entrées

Fish, flesh, and fowl form the basis of the entrée in the Mediterranean diet. Walk through the market at Torre del Greco, the old coral-working town near Naples, and you'll be surprised as razor clams and mussels squirt at you, crabs wave their claws, shrimp are so fresh you expect them to get out of the tub and walk back to the sea, while slabs of swordfish and tuna are taken home to be marinated and sautéed or baked in good oil and herbs.

This passion for seafood is due to the proximity and quality of produce, but is also is the result of the fasting customs of the Church. Lent meant forty days without meat, and Friday meant fish—so much was needed that it was salted, dried, and imported from as far away as Norway as *stockfisk* to Italy and *bacalao* to Spain.

Meat was expensive and prized. A cow or an ox was more use as a puller of ploughs or the giver of milk than being bred for the pot. That was the fate of smaller beasts, such as sheep, goats, and that smallholder's perfect animal, the hog. Every country household had chickens pecking around the door, to provide a steady supply of eggs and, when they didn't, the sort of highly flavored poultry dish most of us only dream about these days.

There are many delectable versions of fish soup around the Mediterranean—not just the most famous, bouillabaisse, but others from southern France, and also from Italy, Greece, Spain, and North Africa. Each one uses seasonings, herbs, and accompaniments appropriate to the area. I tasted this version in Sorrento, Italy, at Easter.

mediterranean fish soup

la cassola di sorrento

6 lb. fish and shellfish, such as red snapper, halibut, sea bass, squid, clams, and crayfish or large shrimp

20 black peppercorns

a large bunch mixed fresh herbs, such as parsley, rosemary, and marjoram

1¼ cups dry white wine

1¼ cups fish stock or water

2 tablespoons extra virgin olive oil

1 large red onion, sliced

4 garlic cloves, sliced

2 dried red chiles, crushed

4 plum tomatoes, peeled,
or 14 oz. canned chopped tomatoes

4–6 slices of bread, 1 inch thick, toasted

serves 4–6

Chop the fish into 2-inch chunks or, if small, leave whole. Put in a large, flameproof casserole. Add the peppercorns, herbs, wine, and stock. Bring to a boil, then reduce the heat to a gentle simmer, and cover. Cook for 5–6 minutes.

Using a slotted spoon, remove the fish to a plate and keep hot. Measure the broth—there should be about 2 cups or so—if not add extra water. Pour into a pitcher or bowl.

Add the oil, onion, garlic, and chiles to the hot pan, sauté for 2 minutes, then add the tomatoes. Return the fish and broth to the pan. Bring back to simmering and serve ladled over chunks of toasted bread as soup, then ladle out the fish as a stew. Alternatively, serve both at the same time.

Note Try 2 tablespoons freshly grated ginger instead of the chiles. Chiles did not appear in the Mediterranean—or in Asia—until the 16th century: ginger, on the other hand, was brought along the Spice Route to Europe from Asia much earlier, and was known in Apulia from that time, though not of course in its fresh form.

Couscous is probably Berber in origin and is found not only in North Africa, but also in Nice and other areas such as Sicily. In this delicious recipe, originally from Trapani, a generous fish stew is ladled over the aromatic *cuscusu* and the juices add their flavor to its fragrant charms. Modern "instant" or precooked couscous is quick and easy because it needs only moistening and heating—a bonus, because cooking traditional North African couscous requires skill and is very time-consuming.

seafood with couscous

cuscusu trapanese

3 lb. assorted non-oily fish and shellfish, such as haddock, halibut, eel, crayfish, lobster, shrimp, crabs, mussels, and clams

1 teaspoon sea salt

4 garlic cloves, sliced

4 celery stalks, sliced

1 head of fennel, quartered

20 black peppercorns, crushed

12-inch strip of unwaxed orange zest

12-inch strip of unwaxed lemon zest

1 large bunch of wild oregano or thyme, fresh or dried

1–2 tablespoons tomato paste

cuscusu

2½ cups coarse instant couscous

1 onion, sliced

2 green chiles, thinly sliced

2 tablespoons extra virgin olive oil

3 cups boiling seafood stock or hot water

1 teaspoon orange flower water (optional)

freshly squeezed juice of 1 orange

sea salt and freshly ground black pepper

serves 4–6

Cut the fish and shellfish into 1-inch chunks or, if small, leave whole. Put them in a very large flameproof casserole dish, add the salt, garlic, celery, fennel, peppercorns, and 2 cups water and bring to a boil. Stir in the orange and lemon zest, oregano, and enough tomato paste to make the liquid rosy. Reduce the heat to a simmer. Cover and cook for 10 minutes.

To prepare the *cuscusu*, put the couscous, onion, chiles, olive oil, salt, and pepper in a heatproof bowl. Pour in the boiling stock. Stir and leave for 5 minutes to plump up. Stir in the orange flower water. When all the liquid has been absorbed, add the orange juice.

Serve the fish and its broth over the *cuscusu* in deep bowls.

This superb, ancient recipe from Provence excites huge passion and interest. Bouillabaisse consists of fragrant fish chunks (and officially should include rascasse, or scorpion fish, but just use whatever is locally available) poached in a saffron-enhanced broth, with aromatics. The dish is served as two courses: first the broth is spooned over toasted or oven-dried bread croutes topped with *rouille* (rust) sauce, which enriches the soup. Next, the fish is eaten. It is undoubtedly a triumph, so do devote several hours to making it. Have no additional courses other than perhaps green salad, a little goat cheese, and some fresh fruit to finish the feast: it is a huge, grand dish in its own right. Serve with chilled Muscadet, sauvignon blanc, chardonnay, or a chilled Provençal rosé.

bouillabaisse

¼ cup extra virgin olive oil

2 large onions, quartered

2 leeks, cut in 2-inch chunks

4 garlic cloves, chopped

2 large fleshy red tomatoes, peeled and quartered, with seeds squeezed out

a bunch of thyme, about 2 oz.

1 fennel bulb with green tops, quartered

8-inch strip of unwaxed orange zest

2 lb. mixed fish fillets such as halibut, red snapper, sea bass, grouper, or cod, all cut into 1½-inch chunks

2 lb. mixed shellfish, such as small crabs, mussels, clams, and shrimp

4 envelopes powdered saffron or a large pinch of threads

2 recipes aïoli (page 12)

1 lb. small, new potatoes, boiled and drained

1 tablespoon Pernod or Ricard (optional)

¼ cup harissa paste or other hot chile paste

sea salt and freshly ground black pepper

1 baguette, sliced and toasted in the oven to make croutes, to serve

serves 4–6

Heat half the oil in a large, flameproof casserole dish, add the onions, leeks, garlic, and tomatoes and sauté until golden and wilted. Add the thyme, fennel, and orange zest. Add 2 quarts boiling water and the remaining oil, then add the fish and shellfish (except the mussels) and half the saffron.

Return to a boil, reduce the heat, and simmer for 10–12 minutes or until the fish is opaque. Add the mussels and clams, if using, and cook for 3–4 minutes until they open. Discard any that don't.

Pour the pan contents through a colander into a large bowl. Lift out the fish into a large, heated tureen or serving dish. Using a slotted spoon, press down on the onions, fennel, thyme, and tomatoes in the colander, then discard them.

Pour the broth back into the rinsed pan, bring to a boil, and cook over very high heat for 5 minutes until emulsified, then whisk in half the aïoli. Add the hot potatoes and stir in the Pernod, if using. Pour about one-quarter of the mixture over the fish.

Put a toasted or oven-dried croute on the side of each soup bowl, then add a generous spoonful of aïoli to each. Mix the remaining aïoli with the harissa and remaining saffron to create a scarlet rouille sauce. Add a spoonful of rouille to the croutes. Ladle hot soup into each dish.

When the soup is finished, serve the fish and hot potatoes with any remaining aïoli and rouille as additional enrichers and flavorings.

Note Broth, seafood, and croutes are sometimes served at the same time.

Lotte or monkfish is a handsome, rich, meaty fish with a dense, satisfying texture—grouper, haddock, rockfish, sablefish, or tilefish are good substitutes. In the Camargue area of southern France, it is sometimes given a robust treatment with red wine and baby vegetables cooked alongside, which become infused with the complex tastes. Serve with red or rosé wine and crusty bread.

french monkfish in wine
la lotte camarguaise

3 lb. monkfish, skinned and trimmed

4 garlic cloves, crushed to a pulp

freshly grated zest and juice of 1 unwaxed lemon

5 sprigs of rosemary or thyme, plus extra to serve (optional)

2 tablespoons clarified butter

2 tablespoons virgin olive oil

12 small potatoes, halved lengthwise or 6 baby globe artichokes, halved or quartered, or a mixture

1¼ cups robust red wine

⅓ cup fish stock or water

sea salt and freshly ground black pepper

kitchen twine

a metal skewer (optional)

serves 4

Tie up the fish at 1-inch intervals with kitchen twine: this helps keep a good shape. A metal skewer can also be pushed down the length to assist the process.

Rub the garlic pulp and lemon zest all over the surface of the fish. Push the rosemary sprigs under the twine, at intervals, down the length of the fish.

Heat the butter and oil in a flameproof casserole dish. Add the fish and brown on all sides, over moderate heat, for 6–8 minutes. Add the halved potatoes, salt, and pepper, then pour in the wine and stock. Bring to a boil.

Reduce the heat to low, cover the pan, and cook gently for 15–20 minutes or until the fish is firm, dense, and white right through, the vegetables are tender, and the wine is well reduced.

Serve fish from the casserole. Carve the fish in 4–8 slices crosswise and spoon over some of the vegetables and sauce, adding extra rosemary if using.

Mediterranean fish markets are often astonishing in their diversity, with gleaming mounds of sea creatures of every shape and size, sparkling with same-day freshness. In Provence, red mullet or red gurnard might be used in this dish. I have used large red snapper, allowing three fillets for layering and three more for the stuffing. Try to buy well-flavored herbs and authentic olives, because these will hugely affect the flavor of the final dish. Serve with chilled, crisp white or rosé wine and crusty bread.

red snapper en papillote

6 large red snapper fillets, about 1½ lb. total

1 teaspoon sea salt

1–2 teaspoons cayenne pepper or Tabasco sauce

3 cups fresh baguette or brioche crumbs

finely grated zest and freshly squeezed juice of 1 large unwaxed orange

6 oz. salt-cured or dry-cured black or green olives, pitted and chopped

4 teaspoons chopped chives, oregano, or thyme

¼ cup extra virgin olive oil

6 anchovies, chopped

a sheet of wax paper, 16 inches square

kitchen twine

a baking sheet

serves 4

Pat 3 of the fillets dry with paper towels and line them up in a row, skin sides down. Season well with sea salt and cayenne pepper.

Put the remaining fillets on a board and chop into small pieces. Put in a food processor, add the bread crumbs, orange zest, olives, and chives. Chop in 5–6 brief bursts until well mixed.

Put the wax paper on a work surface and lay several lengths of kitchen twine across the paper. Add a fish fillet skin side down. Add half the chopped fish mixture, then add another fillet. Add the remaining fish mixture and top with the last fish fillet, skin side up.

Tie the pieces of twine around the fish "sandwich."

Add about 2 tablespoons orange juice and 1 tablespoon of the oil. Fold and twist the paper package to close it securely. Set on the baking tray and bake in a preheated oven at 400°F for 18–20 minutes or until the package has puffed up and the fish smells aromatic. Remove from the oven and set aside.

Meanwhile, put the remaining orange juice, anchovies, and the remaining oil in a blender and pulse to a sharp, salty dressing. Alternatively, use a mortar and pestle.

Unwrap the package. Spoon the dressing over the fish, cut into 4, and serve.

This famous Sicilian fish dish is best made with a tail piece (the *coda*) of fresh tuna, but you can use any large dense portion of the right weight. It must be skinless, boneless, and perfectly trimmed. Tuna cooks to a dense texture: although this dish is not rare-cooked, do try to cook it just until set, so that it is still moist and delicious. Serve with crisp flatbreads or sliced country bread. A lively, fruity, dry white wine would suit.

sicilian tuna

coda di tonno alla tarantelle

3½–4 lb. boneless, skinless, trimmed tail section of fresh tuna

8 garlic cloves, 4 chopped then mashed, 4 left whole

1 unwaxed lemon, zest removed in ½-inch strips

24 sprigs of mint or leaves, plus extra to serve

2 tablespoons unsalted butter

¼ cup extra virgin olive oil

about 28 oz. canned tomatoes in tomato juice (two 14 oz. cans)

¼ cup fish stock

¼ cup white wine

16 small pearl onions

sea salt and freshly ground black pepper

serves 6–8

Pat the tuna dry with paper towels. Slice the 4 whole garlic cloves into 6 long strips each, making 24. Cut the lemon zest into 24 pieces. Starting from the center top, cut a series of 8 incisions in the fish, with a small, sharp knife and keep the point in position while you push a strip of garlic, a mint sprig, and a bit of zest into each incision.

Repeat the process twice more along each side making 2 further rows of incisions and filling them as described. Using your fingers or a pastry brush, rub the mashed garlic over the surface of the fish.

Heat the butter and oil in a large flameproof casserole and brown the tuna all over for 10 minutes, using tongs to position it. Add the tomatoes, their juice, and fish stock and bring to a boil. Cover the pan, reduce the heat, and simmer for 10 minutes. Add the white wine and pearl onions and cook for 15 minutes longer. Remove the fish, keep it warm, and let rest.

Bring the tomato liquid to a boil over high heat, and cook, stirring often, until it has reduced to a thick, rich, red sauce. Add salt and pepper to taste. If you like, put it in a blender and purée until smooth.

Return the fish to its sauce in the casserole for almost 10 minutes or until heated through. Remove it and carve into ½-inch slices. Serve on a bed of tomato sauce with extra mint leaves on top.

Note Serve the extra sauce with rice, pasta, or gnocchi, as a separate course, before or after this course, or the next day.

Squid crops up in every Mediterranean cuisine, prized as much for its simple, sweet, aniseed flavor as for its availability. There are tiny and large squid, but the best for this recipe are about 8 inches long. Allow four per person. If you can't find fresh squid, thawed frozen squid work well, but do not be tempted to buy prepared white squid tubes—they are not ideal for this delicious Italian dish, which needs all the intrinsic fresh flavors. The pretty mauve pigmentation adds color and flavor: do not remove it but let it enhance the dish.

stuffed squid
seppie ripiene ai gamberetti

1 lb. squid, about 8 inches long

12 oz. peeled uncooked shrimp, chopped

a large handful of fresh flat-leaf parsley, plus extra to serve

finely grated zest and freshly squeezed juice of 1 unwaxed lemon

4 garlic cloves, thinly sliced

2 tablespoons salted capers, chopped

¼ cup extra virgin olive oil

⅓ cup medium dry white wine

2 tablespoons Pernod or Ricard

sea salt and freshly ground black pepper

wooden toothpicks

serves 4

To prepare the squid, pull off and separate the tentacles from the body section. Trim off the tentacles whole, then discard the rest. Pull out and discard the transparent quill from each squid tube. Rinse the tubes.

To make the stuffing mixture, chop half the tentacles and mix with the shrimp, parsley, zest, and half the garlic. Stir in the capers, salt, and pepper. Divide the mixture into 16 portions and push some stuffing inside each squid tube. Secure with a wooden toothpick.

Heat the oil in a large skillet. Add the remaining garlic and the stuffed squid and sauté for 2–3 minutes. Pour in the lemon juice, wine, and Pernod, then cover with a lid, reduce the heat, and let simmer for a further 3–4 minutes, turning the squid once, until the filling is cooked (open one to check). Do not overcook or the squid will be tough. Serve hot with a trickle of sauce and extra parsley.

Note If you are unable to buy squid with tentacles, by one extra tube and chop it up to make the stuffing.

This now-grand Spanish rice dish, once a poor man's food from Albufera in Valencia, is made in countless variations in different areas, depending on local ingredients and styles. Traditional combinations also include rabbit with snails—hardly seen outside Spain. Pork ribs with cauliflower and beans is another, and an all-vegetable paella is also popular these days. Use hard, stubby, calasparra rice (sometimes labeled simply "paella rice" in supermarkets) and don't stir it constantly like risotto. The tomato-saffron mix is integral to the dish. Many aficionados maintain that paella tastes best cooked outdoors over a wood fire in a traditional paella or two-handled skillet. However, any version tastes good: a delicious dish.

paella

8 chicken drumsticks and thighs, mixed, or 1 whole chicken, about 3 lb., cut into pieces

2 teaspoons salt

freshly ground black pepper

4 teaspoons smoked paprika or paprika

¼ cup extra virgin olive oil

3–4 boneless pork chops, or 12 oz. salt pork cut into 1-inch cubes

2 onions, chopped

4 garlic cloves, crushed

1 lb. tomatoes, fresh or canned, peeled, seeded, and chopped (14 oz. can)

2 large pinches of saffron threads, or 3 envelopes ground saffron

1¾ cups calasparra (paella) rice

3–3½ cups boiling chicken stock or water

1 cup shelled fresh peas, or frozen and thawed

6 oz. green beans, halved

8 baby artichokes, halved lengthwise, or canned or marinated equivalent

8 large uncooked shrimp, shell on

serves 4–6

Pat the chicken dry with paper towels. Put the salt, pepper, and paprika in a bowl and mix well. Sprinkle the chicken with half the mixture and toss well.

Heat the oil in a large, shallow skillet. Add the chicken and pork, in batches if necessary, and sauté over medium heat for 10–12 minutes or until well browned. Remove with a slotted spoon and set aside.

Add the onions, garlic, tomatoes, and saffron to the pan, then add the remaining salt and paprika. Cook until thickened, about 5 minutes. Stir the mixture well, then replace the meats and stir in the rice and most of the hot stock. Cook over high heat until bubbling fiercely, then reduce the heat and simmer gently, uncovered, for 15 minutes.

Add the peas, beans, artichokes, shrimp, and remaining stock, if necessary, and continue to cook for 10–15 minutes more or until the rice is cooked and glossy but dry. Serve the paella straight from the pan, with cold white or rosé wine.

In Greece *stifado* (or *stifatho*) can refer to a number of things, but essentially it is a thickened stew with tomato and garlic and olive oil—perfect for winter. Sometimes made with beef or rabbit, guinea fowl, or even quail, it is a handsome dish, easy to prepare, and fragrant with herbs. The flambé is an unusual touch—entirely optional, but fun, especially if you use a pleasant, fruity Metaxa brandy. Serve from the dish, accompanied with torn country bread, noodles, rice or even, oddly, with chips.

greek chicken stifado

stifado kotopolou ke elies

3 lb. chicken, whole or quartered, or 4 breast or leg portions

2 tablespoons extra virgin olive oil

10 whole cloves

20 pearl onions or 10 shallots, halved

8 small potatoes, quartered

4 garlic cloves, chopped

2 tablespoons white wine vinegar or lemon juice

⅓ cup rich tomato paste (double strength)

14 oz. canned chopped tomatoes

24 black olives, such as Kalamata

a large bunch fresh or dried rosemary, oregano, thyme, or a mixture

2 tablespoons Greek Metaxa brandy (optional)

freshly ground black pepper

serves 4

Pat the chicken dry with paper towels. Heat the olive oil in a large flameproof casserole dish, add the chicken, and sauté for 8–10 minutes, turning it with tongs from time to time.

Push the cloves into some of the onions and add them all to the pan. Add the potatoes, garlic, vinegar, tomato paste, canned tomatoes, olives, and freshly ground black pepper. Tuck in the herb sprigs around the edges.

Bring to a boil and reduce the heat to low. Cover and simmer for 30 minutes, or about 60 minutes for a whole bird—or until the chicken seems tender and the sauce has reduced and thickened.

Heat the brandy in a warmed ladle and pour it, flaming, over the stifado, then serve.

Note If you have access to a wine merchant who sells Greek wine, try the unusual mavrodaphne, sweet, red and almost port-like.

The Camargue area of southern France is an area of outstanding beauty and has fascinating pools, lagoons, and natural salt-pans surrounded by wild grasses and inhabited by pink flamingos and wild white horses. The red rice from this region, justly famous, takes over twice the usual time to cook but is good served with hearty wine and other intense tastes, as in this easy chicken dish.

camargue chicken
with red rice

- 4 boneless chicken breasts, preferably free-range, or 4 chicken quarters
- 2 tablespoons salted butter
- ¼ cup virgin olive oil
- 2 garlic cloves, chopped
- 1¼ cups Camargue red rice (see note)
- 2 cups boiling chicken stock
- 3 leeks, white parts sliced into 2-inch chunks, green tops finely sliced
- ½ cup robust white wine
- 6 slices smoked bacon or pancetta, whole or cut into strips
- 2 tablespoons tarragon vinegar
- 30–40 fresh tarragon leaves (optional)
- sea salt and freshly ground black pepper

serves 4

Pat the chicken breasts dry with paper towels and cut 2 slashes on top of each.

Heat half the butter and all the oil in a large flameproof casserole dish and brown the chicken, skin side first, until golden and aromatic. Remove from the pan and set aside.

Add the garlic and rice to the pan and stir over high heat for 1 minute. Pour in the chicken stock and 1¼ cups boiling water. Add the white part of the leeks, salt, and pepper. Cover the pan and cook over low heat for 3 minutes. Uncover the pan, then add the chicken pieces, pushing them into the rice. Add the white wine and put the bacon on top.

Increase the heat slightly. Cover the pan again and cook for another 10–12 minutes, then add the tarragon vinegar, the fresh tarragon, and the green part of the leeks. Cook for a final 5 minutes, uncover the pan, and add the remaining butter, tilting the pan to mix.

Serve hot with the same wine used in cooking.

Note If red rice is unavailable, you could substitute wild rice, but presoak it for 2 hours in hot (not boiling) water to shorten the cooking time. Drain, then proceed as above.

Greek bakers have traditionally allowed villagers to use the fading heat of their bread ovens to cook the Sunday lunch, and many Mediterranean households cook without having their own oven, or have an outdoor oven used only on feast days and special occasions. This recipe suits this sort of treatment. Chicken is cooked with noodles and a rich tomato sauce which is soaked up by the noodles. It becomes crusty on top and very succulent. The cinnamon, probably a centuries-old Turkish influence, is now appreciated and even considered a Greek norm. So is the added sweetness: an interesting touch. *Paximathia*, twice-cooked bread, is a Greek pantry standby. Look for it in Greek or Cypriot stores or use any good-quality bread, sliced and oven-dried. Serve with a salad of baby lettuce and cucumber, dressed with cold-pressed extra virgin olive oil and Greek Kalamata olives.

greek chicken with noodles

kotopolou ke hilopittes

3 lb. chicken or 2½ lb. guinea fowl, without giblets

2 tablespoons extra virgin olive oil, plus extra cold-pressed to serve

a small bunch of dried oregano

3 red bell peppers, quartered and seeded

2 onions, sliced

2 cinnamon sticks, crushed

10 oz. *hilopittes* (dried flat Greek ribbon noodles) or fettuccine

1 tablespoon sugar

4 fresh or dried bay leaves, bruised

28 oz. canned plum tomatoes (two 14. oz. cans)

¼ cup dried bread crumbs, such as paximathia or dried rusks, crushed to crumbs (optional)

⅓ cup freshly grated kefalotyri or Parmesan cheese

sea salt and freshly ground black pepper

to serve

salad of green leaves and cucumber

Kalamata olives

serves 4

Rub the chicken all over with some of the olive oil, then sprinkle with salt, pepper, and half the dried oregano. Put in a large, heavy roasting pan. Pack the bell peppers, onions, and cinnamon around the bird, then add the noodles.

Put the sugar, bay leaves, tomatoes, and their juice and the remaining oregano in a saucepan, add 1–1¼ cups boiling water and heat to boiling point. Pour evenly around the chicken, then sprinkle the remaining olive oil over the top.

Roast in a preheated oven at 350°F for 1¼–1½ hours or until the bird is fairly tender, the pasta nearly cooked, and most of the tomato juice absorbed. (If necessary sprinkle ¼–⅓ cup water over the noodles, or cover with aluminum foil to prevent it drying out.)

Remove from the oven, then sprinkle with the bread crumbs and cheese. Roast for a further 20–30 minutes or until everything is well cooked and very tender.

Serve the chicken, noodles, and sauce directly from the pan, all in one.

Duck with olives has always been a famous Spanish, French, and Italian delicacy, and both main ingredients are often of high quality in all three countries. Instead of using a whole duck, cut into pieces, this recipe uses "magrets" or boneless breast portions. The skin is left on but is slashed so it browns well and some of the delicious duck fat adds richness to the sauce. Choose green olives, either unpitted or ready-stuffed—the effect is subtle but satisfying. Pedro Ximenez is a superb, rare, sweet Spanish sherry which can be found at a Spanish gourmet store or specialist vintner. Serve a red Rioja with this dish.

spanish duck with olives

pato con olivas

2 large magrets (boneless breast portions) of muscovy or other duck about 1 lb.

1 teaspoon coarsely crushed black pepper

½ teaspoon sea salt

4 garlic cloves, finely chopped then crushed

8 shallots or pearl onions

2 tablespoons sherry vinegar

⅓ cup Pedro Ximenez sherry or other aged sweet sherry, or ¼ cup pomegranate molasses

40 whole, or pitted and stuffed green olives (with anchovies, lemon zest, or almonds)

¼ cup chicken or beef consommé, or rich stock

1½ cups cooked (or canned) white beans, lentils or chickpeas, drained (two 14 oz. cans)

2 tablespoons fresh herbs, such as parsley and celery tops

serves 4

Preheat a ridged, stove-top grill pan until very hot. Pat the duck breasts dry with paper towels.

Mix the pepper and salt and half the garlic to a paste. Rub some all over the duck breasts. Make 3 diagonal slashes on the skin side of each breast, then cook skin side down for 2 minutes. Reduce the heat to moderate and continue to cook until the fat runs and the surface is darkly browned.

Pour out and reserve the fat, returning 1 tablespoon to the pan. Using tongs, turn the duck breasts over. Add the shallots and sherry. Cover and cook over low heat for a further 4–6 minutes or until the duck is rare or medium-rare, depending on your taste.

Add the olives and another tablespoon of duck fat to the sauce. Remove the duck breasts and keep them warm. Add the consommé to the pan, then shake and stir until the sauce becomes a rich, syrupy glaze.

Put the beans in a saucepan and crush coarsely with a fork or potato masher. Stir in 2 tablespoons of the duck fat, salt, pepper, herbs, and the remaining garlic and heat through.

Cut the duck crosswise or diagonally into thin slices. Serve with a trickle of sauce and a mound of the mashed beans.

This recipe, modeled on the more usual veal escalopes with Marsala, is easy to make with pork tenderloins, cut into small oval escalopes or *scaloppine*. Serve with side dishes such as buttered spinach or tiny roasted potatoes, and a soft red wine, a glass of the same Marsala used in the sauce, or a dry Marsala.

pork tenderloin with marsala

scaloppine di maiale al marsala

1½–2 pork tenderloins, about 1½ lb.

⅔ cup all-purpose flour

1 teaspoon salt

1 teaspoon ground ginger or grated nutmeg

4 tablespoons salted butter

2 tablespoons extra virgin olive oil

¼ cup blanched almonds, flaked or whole

⅓ cup sweet Marsala wine

2 tablespoons jellied veal or beef stock, or canned beef or chicken consommé

serves 4

Cut the tenderloins crosswise into ½-inch slices. Cut each slice almost through again, then open out and press flat with the heel of your palm. You should have about 24 flattened butterflied pieces or *scaloppine*.

Sift the flour, salt, and ginger together onto a flat plate. Press 6 pieces of pork into this mixture until well coated on both sides.

Put half the butter and half the oil in a nonstick skillet and heat until sizzling. Cook the almonds briefly until golden, then remove with a slotted spoon and set aside. Add 6 of the prepared *scaloppine* to the pan and cook for 2 minutes each side, pressing them down well, then use tongs to remove, and keep hot. Continue with a second batch of 6.

Add half the Marsala to the pan and stir to dissolve the sediment. Pour into a bowl and keep it warm. Wash and dry the pan.

Using the remaining butter and oil, repeat the process until the second batch of pork is cooked. Keep hot in the same way.

Pour the remaining Marsala into the pan, then add the jellied meat stock or consommé. Scrape, stir, and heat until well dissolved, then add the reserved warm pan sauce made earlier. Heat again until sticky and intensely flavored. Return the pork to the pan and turn it in the hot sauce.

Serve 6 *scaloppine* per person, with a generous spoonful of the rich, sticky Marsala glaze and the nuts.

Loukanika (Greece) and *luganega* (Italy) are similar types of sausage and have been known since antiquity. They contain fresh, coarsely cut pork and/or ground beef with salt, sugar, orange, chile, cumin or aniseed, and coriander, with plenty of garlic, red wine, and olive oil. This is all packed inside a long, traditional sausage casing and often sold coiled into a spiral. The sausages are then pan-fried, roasted, grilled, or broiled to a succulent golden brown. Buy them at Italian specialty shops, but if unavailable, you could substitute any dense, coarsely textured, spicy Italian link sausages (not the same, but acceptable). Luganega also makes a great addition to the barbecue.

luganega country sausage
with lentils and wilted greens

3 tablespoons extra virgin olive oil

1 lb. luganega coarse-cut spicy pork spiral

1½ cups canned Italian lentils, pinto, cannellini, or lima beans (two 14 oz. cans)

4 garlic cloves, chopped

1 onion, grated

1 lb. arugula or flat leaf parsley, washed and shaken dry

2 tablespoons dry vermouth or white wine

sea salt and freshly ground black pepper

serves 4

Heat half the olive oil in a heavy skillet, add the sausage, and sauté over moderate heat for 6–8 minutes or until very hot, browned, and firm. Drain and discard the liquid from the pan. Keep the sausage hot over very low heat.

Meanwhile pour the lentils and their liquid into a saucepan and cook for 5 minutes or until very hot, then drain, discarding most of the liquid. Add salt, pepper, garlic, onion, and the remaining oil and stir over medium heat.

Put the arugula in the pan with the hot sausage. Add the vermouth and cook briefly, covered, until the leaves are vividly green and wilted. Serve the sausages on lentils with the wilted greens alongside or on top.

Souvlaki is the Greek equivalent of the kabob, a street food traditionally eaten at festival time. These days, it is mostly made of pork (though lamb is used when in season). Loved by locals and travelers alike, it is inexpensive, filling and delicious, with its pungent yogurt, garlic, and cucumber dressing and hot, soft pita bread. In Greece, the local bread is often briefly pan-fried; at home it is better to brush pita bread with oil and water and bake briefly, or put under the broiler until heated through. Though pita bread comes from the Middle East, not Greece, it "pockets" beautifully, making the perfect receptacle for a meat and salad snack.

souvlaki in pita

4 large pita breads

water and olive oil, to moisten the bread

2 teaspoons chopped fresh oregano, or 1 teaspoon dried oregano, crushed

2 tablespoons freshly squeezed lemon juice

½ onion, coarsely grated

2 tablespoons extra virgin olive oil

1 lb. lean pork or lamb (usually leg meat), cut into ½-inch cubes

salad, such as:

lettuce or cabbage, finely sliced

cucumber, sliced

red bell pepper, sliced

tomatoes, cut into wedges

radishes, halved

red onion, sliced into rings

garlic dressing

⅓ cup plain yogurt, drained

4 garlic cloves, chopped and crushed

2 inches cucumber, coarsely grated, then squeezed dry

½ teaspoon sea salt

metal skewers

serves 4

Brush or sprinkle the pita breads all over with the water and oil and either broil or bake in a preheated oven at 350°F for 3–5 minutes or long enough to soften the bread, but not dry it. Cut off a strip from the long side, then pull open and part the sides of the breads to make a pocket. Push the strip inside. Keep the breads warm.

Put the oregano, lemon juice, onion, and olive oil in a bowl and mash with a fork. Add the cubed meat and toss well. Cover and let marinate for 10–20 minutes. Drain, then thread the meat onto metal skewers. Cook on a preheated outdoor grill or stove-top grill pan for 5–8 minutes, or until golden outside and cooked through.

Put your choice of salad ingredients in a bowl, toss gently, then insert into the pockets of the pita breads.

To make the dressing, put the yogurt in a bowl, then beat in the garlic, cucumber, and salt. Add a large spoonful to each pocket.

Remove the hot, cooked meat from the skewers, then push it into the pockets. Serve immediately, while the meat and bread are hot and the salad cool.

Note Alternatively, you can roll the warm flatbread around the filling in a cone shape—a more common method in Greece. Unusually, they sometimes add fries to the cone as well, before wrapping in wax paper.

Liver, along with other kinds of variety meats, has always been a delicacy in Mediterranean kitchens, especially in Greece, Italy, and Spain, where it can be served as a kabob, an appetizer, or an entrée. It is often cooked simply, with few spices or herbs. Lamb's liver, in small pieces, or halved chicken livers are both appropriate for this recipe. Herb-flavored rice and seasonal greens, cooked then dressed with olive oil and a squeeze of lemon, are typical accompaniments.

chicken liver and bacon wraps
sikotti apo zante

12 oz. chicken livers or lamb's liver

1 nutmeg

8 thin slices bacon, halved lengthwise

2 tablespoons extra virgin olive oil

⅓ cup red wine or sweet red vermouth

¼ cup tomato purée

¼ cup chicken or lamb stock or water

sea salt and freshly ground black pepper

toothpicks

serves 4

Use kitchen shears to cut whole chicken livers into 2–4 pieces, discarding the membranous parts or any discolored areas. If using lamb's liver, cut it ½ inch thick and then into 1-inch pieces. Pat dry with paper towels and dust with salt and pepper. Coarsely grate half the nutmeg and sprinkle over the liver, then wrap the bacon strips around each pair of liver pieces, securing them with toothpicks.

Heat the oil in a large, nonstick skillet and sauté the liver and bacon wraps for 1½–2 minutes on each side or until the bacon fat is translucent, the liver golden, and the texture firm, but not hard. Push the meat to one side of the pan.

Put the remaining nutmeg piece in the pan with the wine, tomato purée, and stock. Cook, stirring over medium heat to dissolve the sediment on the base of the pan, to make a sauce. Turn the liver briefly in the sauce and reheat gently for 1 minute, then serve.

A Provençal daube of beef is a grand, classic stew, left bubbling for hours, enriched with a slice of pork or bacon rind, and fragrant with red wine. This simplified version is easy and straightforward, so there's time to make the aromatic lemon, parsley, and garlic topping, called *gremolata* (not Provençal but Italian). Traditionally, this is served with the Italian dish *osso buco*, but it has been known to migrate west into French dishes—a familiar Mediterranean tendency. The lemon flesh adds additional vibrancy to the dish. Serve with a rich, substantial red wine, such as Cahors.

provençal beef daube
with lemon and parsley

2 lb. beef round steak, cut 1 inch thick

2 tablespoons extra virgin olive oil

10 garlic cloves, sliced

8 oz. slab bacon, cubed

2 red onions, quartered

4 medium carrots, left whole

6 plum tomatoes, cut into wedges

zest of 1 unwaxed lemon removed with a lemon zester

1 fresh bouquet garni of thyme, bay, parsley, and oregano, tied with kitchen twine,

3 oz. prunes, about ¾ cup

1 cup rich red wine, such as Cahors

¾ cup boiling beef stock

a bunch of flat-leaf parsley, freshly chopped

⅓ cup fresh brioche or bread crumbs (optional)

sea salt and freshly ground black pepper

serves 4

Beat the beef all over with a meat hammer or rolling pin, then cut it into 2-inch square chunks. Heat the oil in a large, flameproof casserole dish, add the beef, in batches if necessary, and sauté for 4 minutes on each side. Remove with a slotted spoon and set aside.

Add 2 of the garlic cloves to the pan, then add the bacon, onions, and carrots. Stir and sauté until the bacon is golden and the fat has run. Add the tomatoes, half the lemon zest, the bouquet garni, prunes, wine, and stock. Replace the browned beef, pushing the pieces well down under the liquid.

Remove and discard the white pith from the lemon. Cut the flesh into tiny cubes and add to the pan—they give flavor and tenderness to the meat.

Reduce the heat to a gentle simmer. Cover with a lid and cook, undisturbed, for 1½ hours, then test for doneness. (If preferred, cook in a low oven at 325°F for 2½ hours or until tender.)

To make the gremolata, chop the remaining garlic, and mix with the remaining lemon zest, the parsley, and bread crumbs.

Serve the daube with a little of its sauce and the gremolata sprinkled on top. (The rest can be served over pasta or rice, as another course or later meal.)

CHILO

salads and vegetables

Salads and vegetables, in Mediterranean tradition, are served separately. Such 'accompaniments' are not heaped ignominiously onto a plate with everything else. Instead, they are accorded the dignity they deserve.

Salads served at the start of a Mediterranean meal must amuse the eye and curiosity, but not kill the appetite. Some can be served as a main dish in their own right, but most often salads come after the entrée, or are served with it, but separately. In Italian, Greek, and Spanish meals, a selection of small, salad-like dishes can make up the antipasto, meze, tapas, or starter course. In Provence, as in the rest of France, a salad often comes at the end of a meal, with the cheese, before a final sweet dish. Sometimes it may be as simple as some raw fennel, celery, or chicory with coarse salt and pepper, at other times it will be a classic green leaf and herb salad.

On Italian menus, vegetables are listed under contorni and arrive in separate bowls. In Greece, they are served like meze, in separate small dishes or bowls, in Spain, they are served as tapas or the main dish, while in Provence, they are served as a separate course, as in the rest of France.

Misticanza and mesclun are just two of the charming names given to young herb and leaf salads in Italy and Provence. They are regularly gathered, wild, from spring hillsides and fields. They should contain a good mix of peppery, sweet, mild, sharp, and slightly bitter or astringent leaves. These days, enterprising farmers' markets and supermarkets sell them ready-mixed, so buy theirs or assemble your own, allowing about one-and-a-half handfuls per person. Sometimes a crust of baguette is rubbed well with fresh garlic to scent the salad, and set at the bottom of the salad bowl—this is called a *chapon*. Other times, toasted or pan-grilled bread, sprinkled with oil, rubbed with garlic and salt, is added: one per person, rather like crostini or bruschetta. To this salad, shavings of hard cheese, such as pecorino, and hot red pepper flakes can be added. Use your best olive oil and most delicious light vinegar for the dressing: simple, perfect, and classic.

mixed green salad
insalata misticanza

2 handfuls bitter baby leaves such as frisée, red chard, or endive

2 handfuls of crisp, mild, sweet baby leaves such as oakleaf or romaine hearts

2 handfuls of peppery herb leaves such as watercress or arugula

a handful of aromatic herbs such as mint, tarragon, chives, flat-leaf parsley, dill, chervil, or basil

1 red onion, finely sliced

4 slices fresh baguette (½-inch thick), broiled, pan-grilled, or grilled on one side

2 large garlic cloves, unpeeled and crushed

1 tablespoon olive oil

a pinch of sea salt

dressing

⅓ cup first cold-pressed extra virgin olive oil

1½ tablespoons white or red wine vinegar

½–1 teaspoon crumbled hot red pepper flakes (optional)

a pinch of sea salt

serves 4

Wash the salad and herb leaves and onion slices in cold water, spin or pat dry, then put in a large plastic bag and seal tightly. Chill for 30 minutes to 4 hours until ready to serve.

To make the croutes, rub the cooked surfaces of the bread with the garlic flesh, making a generous layer. Trickle 1 tablespoon of oil on top, then add a pinch of salt.

To make the dressing put the ⅓ cup oil, the vinegar, chilli flakes, if using, and salt in a bowl or bottle, and whisk or shake to form an emulsified dressing.

When ready to serve, pour the dressing into a large salad bowl or 4 small ones. Pile the salad lightly on top, but do not toss. Tuck in the garlicky croutes. Toss well until gleaming and serve immediately.

As summer turns towards fall, and winter weather looms, it is the red-leafed salad stuffs that become more prominently displayed in many French produce stores. In Provençal towns, another colorful local vegetable is red-stemmed Swiss chard or *blettes*. The people of Nice often even describe themselves as "chard eaters" or *kaka blettes*, because it is such an important part of the local diet: in Menton's main square it is planted decoratively, in pride of place, as part of an ornamental garden. When mature, chard is always eaten cooked, in tartes, tians, and thick omelets, such as *trouchia*. Chefs include the tiny, immature leaves with other little red leaves for its refreshing, mildly astringent taste. As for all salad making, try to combine a balance of crisp and soft with sweet and bitter. Pumpkin seeds and pumpkin seed oil, both part of traditional cuisine, seem to be back in fashion. Look for dark, sticky, roasted pumpkin seed oil in gourmet stores, and use it quickly because it won't keep well after opening. Alternatively keep in the coolest, darkest part of the refrigerator.

red leaf salad
salade rouge

2 small heads of radicchio (round shaped)
2 heads pointed red Belgian endive
2 heads Italian-style pointed red escarole
¼–½ head of red oakleaf lettuce
2 handfuls baby red chard leaves
1 tablespoon extra virgin olive oil
¼ cup husked pumpkin seeds
1 red onion, cut into fine segments or rings

dressing

3 tablespoons extra virgin olive oil
¼ cup roasted pumpkin seed oil or extra virgin olive oil
1 tablespoon red wine or sherry vinegar
2 teaspoons Dijon mustard
1 tablespoon crème de cassis (optional)
sea salt and freshly ground black pepper

serves 4

Wash the radicchio, chicory, escarole, lettuce, and chard and separate into leaves. Spin dry in a salad spinner.

Put the 1 tablespoon olive oil in a skillet, add the pumpkin seeds, and toss over low heat until toasted and aromatic. Take care, because they can burn easily. Remove from the heat and let cool on a plate.

To make the dressing, put the olive and pumpkin seed oils in a salad bowl, add the vinegar, mustard, crème de cassis, if using, salt, and pepper, and beat with a fork until emulsified.

Add the leaves, red onion, and pumpkin seeds, toss well, then serve.

The green bean salad, especially served warm, is a classic French dish with many variations. Pickled versions have echoes of the cooking of Ancient Greece and Rome: the vinaigrette has sweet wine and lightly crushed coriander seeds along with other sweet-sour items. This style of recipe is often referred to as *à la grecque*, which means made with olive oil and lemon—not surprising, looking at the history of this region.

provençal pickled beans

4 oz. tiny pickling onions or other pearl onions

12 oz. green beans, stemmed

2 tablespoons currants, golden raisins, or raisins

1 lemon, halved

⅓ cup extra virgin olive oil

2 tablespoons sweet wine, such as Muscat

1 tablespoon balsamic or red wine vinegar

2 teaspoons pomegranate molasses, plus extra to serve (optional)

1 fresh or dried red or green chile, sliced or crumbled

1 teaspoon coriander seeds, lightly crushed

sea salt and freshly ground black pepper

serves 4

Put the onions, beans, and currants in a saucepan, add a pinch of salt, and cover with boiling water. Simmer until the onions are barely soft and the beans are bright green and snap-tender. Drain, refresh in cold water, and pat dry.

Squeeze the juice from half the lemon, then put it in a bowl or jar with the oil, wine, vinegar, molasses, if using, chile, and coriander seeds, then beat or shake to mix. Add salt and pepper to taste. Beat or shake again, then pour over the vegetables.

Serve, if possible, still warm, and trickle extra pomegranate molasses, if using, on top. Cut the remaining lemon into wedges and add to each serving.

Variation Add 1 teaspoon tomato paste or sun-dried tomato paste to the vinaigrette dressing.

Popular in France and Italy, mâche grows as a tiny rosette of leaves. Now cultivated, it used to be picked from the wild in fall, and has always been associated with other autumnal ingredients, including walnuts and beets. Don't overmix, or the egg, which would otherwise be a fetching rosy pink, become rather lurid. So go gently.

mâche with beets

2 large handfuls of the pale inner leaves from frisée, pulled into pieces

1 large handful of mâche or lamb's lettuce, well washed and trimmed

1 white onion, finely sliced

4 cooked baby beets, peeled

¼ cup extra virgin olive oil

2 tablespoons freshly squeezed lemon juice

1–2 tablespoons walnut or hazelnut oil

½ teaspoon sea salt

1 teaspoon cracked black peppercorns

1 hard-cooked egg, chopped

2 tablespoons tiny capers, drained

serves 4

Wash the salad leaves and onion slices, then spin dry in a salad spinner. If you have time, put them in a large plastic bag, seal it, and chill for 30 minutes or up to 4 hours.

Cut the beets into batons, cubes, or chunks. Put them in a bowl and toss them in half the olive oil and stir in the lemon juice, nut oil, salt, and peppercorns. Set aside.

At serving time, put the salad leaves in a bowl or bowls. Sprinkle with the beet pieces and their dressing, then dot with the egg. Heat the remaining olive oil and the capers in a small skillet until sizzling and hissing. Trickle directly over the salad and serve immediately.

Variation Add 2 tablespoons broken walnut pieces to the capers and oil. Sizzle and pour over, as above.

This Arab-influenced salad probably came to the south of France with immigrants from North Africa, or perhaps much earlier with traders from the Middle East, or the Moors to Spain. Try to use young, tender fennel bulbs, and choose vividly juicy and colorful oranges (or try it with minneolas, clementines, satsumas, or mandarins). To cut off all of the bitter pith, slice a piece off the top and base of each fruit, then slice off the skin and white pith from top to bottom using a fine, serrated vegetable knife, in a sawing movement—easy and effective. Orange flower water is sold in Italian and Middle Eastern shops.

fennel and orange salad

5 large unwaxed oranges, about 1½ lb., or equivalent weight of minneolas, clementines, satsumas, or mandarins, washed and dried

1–2 heads of young fennel, preferably with green tops

2 red onions, finely sliced

24 black olives, preferably the dry-cured Provençal type

dressing

¼ cup extra virgin olive oil

½ teaspoon orange-flower water or 1 tablespoon orange juice or zest

1 teaspoon sea salt

½ teaspoon white, green, or pink peppercorns, well crushed or chopped

serves 4

Using a vegetable peeler, remove the zest of 1 orange or 2 smaller citrus fruits, then slice the zest into thin strips. Alternatively use a zester or canelle knife. Set aside. Halve and squeeze the juice from the zested fruit into a bowl.

Remove a slice from the top and bottom of the remaining fruit then prepare as described in the recipe introduction. Discard the debris. Slice each fruit crosswise into thin rounds, adding any juice to the bowl.

Finely slice the fennel bulb lengthwise. Toss it immediately in the bowl of juice. Assemble the fennel, oranges, onions, and olives on a flat salad platter, then add the reserved zest and pour the juice over the top.

To make the dressing, put the olive oil, orange-flower water, salt, and pepper in a bowl or jar and beat or shake well. Pour the dressing over the salad and serve cool.

The famous Salade Niçoise was originally composed of crudités with eggs and anchovies added. Now served in cafés, restaurants, and snack bars from New Zealand to Newfoundland, it is often made badly and bowdlerized. Tuna, too costly for inclusion until recent times, can be fresh or canned, as long as it is of high quality. The anchovies can be salted, canned, or marinated, though marinated is really a Spanish innovation. Although this is a splendid entrée, it is also appealing as a side salad if served in small quantities.

salade niçoise

1 head romaine lettuce, or 3 romaine lettuce hearts, or one crisp iceberg, leaves separated and halved if large

2 scallions or shallots, sliced

8–12 oz. good-quality canned tuna, drained, or belly tuna, broiled or poached, and cut into bite-size pieces

2 oz. canned anchovies, or 24 marinated anchovies, halved lengthwise

12 black olives, such as Niçoise

4 hard-cooked eggs, peeled and quartered

a handful of small sprigs of flat leaf parsley or basil

4 ripe tomatoes, cut into 4–8 wedges

4 oz. green beans, halved, or shelled fava beans, freshly boiled

vinaigrette

2 garlic cloves, crushed to a pulp

½ teaspoon sea salt

2 tablespoons wine vinegar

½ cup first cold-pressed extra virgin olive oil

serves 4

Line a large salad bowl with the lettuce leaves. Add the scallions, tuna, anchovies, olives, egg quarters, parsley, tomatoes, and beans.

To make the vinaigrette, put the garlic, salt, vinegar, and olive oil in a bowl or bottle and beat or shake until emulsified. Pour over the salad just before serving.

Note Purists maintain that there is no place for potatoes in this dish. Although other baby vegetables such as artichoke hearts are acceptable, trivia such as carrots are absolutely unacceptable and wrong.

A famous Spanish dish of summer or fall vegetables roasted to sweetness is deceptively simple and now famous around the world. Its success depends on excellent olive oil and vegetables cooked in their skins for extra flavor. There are many Mediterranean variations of course: in some parts of France and Spain, you will find anchovy strips lining the pepper halves, or fragments of salt cod and sometimes capers, olives, or even cubes of goat cheese. Different herbs can be added at serving time and even a few drops of vinegar, but on the whole simplicity is best. Serve as an accompaniment or as an entrée with bread. Excellent with a fruity white, rosé, or even fino sherry.

spanish roasted vegetables

escalivada

2 red bell peppers, halved lengthwise

2 yellow or orange bell peppers, halved lengthwise

2 red onions

4 slices butternut squash or pumpkin, about ½ inch thick, seeded if necessary, or 2 large zucchini, halved lengthwise, scored with a fork

2 baby eggplant or 1 large, sliced lengthwise and scored with a fork

2 whole garlic heads

⅓–½ cup first cold-pressed extra virgin olive oil

sea salt and freshly ground black pepper

1 small handful of fresh herbs, such as parsley, oregano, mint and thyme

aluminum foil

1–2 roasting pans

serves 4

Leave the stems on the peppers, but remove and discard the pith and seeds. Cut the unpeeled onions almost in half crosswise, leaving one side joined, as a hinge. Remove and discard the seeds and pith from the squash, but leave otherwise intact.

Cut the unpeeled heads of garlic almost in half crosswise, leaving a hinge of papery skin. Pour a teaspoon of the oil over the cut surfaces of the garlic, then put the bulbs back together again. Wrap up in foil, to make 2 packages.

Arrange all the prepared vegetables, including the eggplant, in a single layer in the roasting pan(s), cut sides uppermost. Sprinkle with 3–4 tablespoons of the oil.

Roast in a preheated oven at 475°F for 35–40 minutes or until soft and fragrant. Transfer to a serving dish, sprinkle with the herbs and remaining oil, and serve hot or warm.

A tian is a shallow baking dish, often glazed earthenware. Like the word "casserole," the name has also come to mean the food cooked in it. These days tians usually contain vegetables and herbs and sometimes cheese and eggs. A tian I have eaten in Mougins, for example, was more like a baked omelet than a casserole, almost a crustless quiche. Others may contain a little rice and *petit salé* bacon. This is a delicious version that can be served in spoonfuls or in wedges, with bread, or a salad.

provençal vegetable tian

1 small eggplant, cut into ½-inch cubes

2 teaspoons salt

2 tablespoons extra virgin olive oil

2 tablespoons butter

4 garlic cloves, chopped

1 onion, sliced

4 scallions or 1 baby leek, sliced

1 handful of spinach or Swiss chard, chopped

1 handful of baby asparagus or green beans, cut into 1-inch lengths

8 eggs

1 cup heavy cream or crème fraîche

1 cup grated Parmesan, pecorino, or Gruyère cheese

an earthenware dish, casserole, or metal baking pan

serves 4

Put the eggplant in a plastic or ceramic dish, sprinkle with the 2 teaspoons salt, and set aside for 15 minutes or until all the other ingredients have been prepared.

Heat the oil and 1 tablespoon of the butter in a skillet, add the garlic, onion, scallions, spinach, and asparagus, and sauté over moderate heat for 6–8 minutes, stirring constantly, until the vegetables are soft but still colorful. Remove with a slotted spoon.

Put the eggplant in a colander and let drain—do not wash it. Pat dry with paper towels, removing most of the salt. Add the remaining butter to the skillet, add the eggplant, and sauté for 5 minutes.

Put the eggs, cream, and Parmesan in a bowl and beat with a fork.

Transfer the eggplant, vegetables, and their juices and oil into the tian, distributing them evenly. Pour the egg and cheese mixture over the top and bake in a preheated oven at 400°F for 5 minutes. Reduce the heat to 350°F for a further 20 minutes and cook until set and nicely browned.

Serve hot, warm, or cool.

The great Turkish classic dish, imam bayildi, is similar to this recipe. In Greek, *papoutsakias* means "little shoes" and they do in fact look like slippers. They are often flavored with leaves from the pot of basil seen on Greek window sills, but I have used oregano, that favorite of all Greek herbs. The local kind, known as *rigani*, grows wild everywhere and seems to have more verve than any other variety. Don't be shocked by the amount of garlic and oil, or by the cooking time. Originally the slippers were left to cook for long periods in the cooling heat of a baker's oven—almost to the point of collapse. Serve with chunks of crusty bread and a robust red wine.

stuffed greek eggplant
papoutsakias

2 large eggplant, about 1½ lb., halved lengthwise

⅓ cup extra virgin olive oil

6 garlic cloves, crushed

1 red or white onion, sliced into rings

6 firm-fleshed vine-ripened tomatoes, blanched, peeled, then cut into segments

2 celery stalks (optional)

1 teaspoon dried oregano

¼ cup thick tomato paste

sprigs of fresh oregano, marjoram, or thyme (optional)

4 thin slices cheese, such as Greek kasseri, Cheddar, or pecorino, about 2 oz. (optional)

sea salt and freshly ground black pepper

a baking dish big enough to hold the eggplant in a single layer

serves 4

Using a sharp, serrated knife, cut out the central flesh of the eggplant halves, leaving a ½-inch shell. Cut the flesh into ½-inch chunks. Heat ¼ cup of the oil in a large skillet, then add the garlic and eggplant halves, cut sides down. Cook over moderate heat for 5 minutes. Remove and set the eggplant halves, cut side up, in a baking dish, ready to be filled. Leave the oil and garlic in the pan.

Put the eggplant halves in a preheated oven at 350°F for 15 minutes while you prepare the filling and sauce.

Add the eggplant cubes to the oil in the pan. Sauté for 5 minutes, then add the onion, tomatoes, celery, if using, and the dried oregano to the skillet and cook over high heat. Add the remaining oil and cook, stirring constantly, until the eggplant chunks are fairly soft and the tomatoes reduced. Scoop up the eggplant pieces with some of the other vegetables and pile them inside the partially cooked shells and bake them for a further 40 minutes.

Meanwhile, add the tomato paste to the pan, then add ¾ cup boiling water. Stir over gentle heat for a further 15 minutes to form a rich, soft, fragrant sauce, then turn off the heat. Taste and season well with salt and pepper.

After 1 hour in the oven, test the eggplant: the outer shells should be dark, wrinkled, and soft. If not, cook them for another 20 minutes. Serve the eggplant in their baking dish or a serving plate, with the sauce poured over and around. Top with the fresh herbs and cheese, if using. Serve hot, warm, or cool.

pasta, bread, and pizza

Wheat is the staple of the Mediterranean diet. The Romans of course swore by bread and circuses and waged constant war to keep up the supply of bread to the people. They weren't fascinated only by Cleopatra's bright eyes, but by her endless fields of grain. Egypt was seen as the granary of Rome.

Wheat produces bread of extraordinary diversity, from the leavened bread made by professional bakers, as you find in most of Europe, to the flat, unleavened kind—pita, lavash, and *carta di musica* for instance—a legacy of the periodic Arab domination of parts of the Mediterranean. It has the advantage that it can be cooked on an ordinary stove, and doesn't need the attentions of the professional baker. Baker's dough is used as the base for local versions of the flavored tart found all around the area; pizza in southern Italy, pide in Turkey, pissaladiére in the south of France, or coca in Spain.

It's also wheat that provides the basis of pasta and noodles—in Greece for the egg-based *hilopittes* and the plain *kritharaki*, in France, for vermicelli and macaroni, and in Italy for an endless array of plain or egg-based pasta, fresh or dried, all made with special fine pasta flour, *tipo 00*.

Real Italian pesto is an exuberantly intense, rich paste of garlic, basil, and cheese, given extra texture with pine nuts. Ligurians take pride in this culinary masterpiece: they say that the basil in their part of the Mediterranean has particular pungency. Pesto must be made and eaten fresh: heat-treated pesto, sold in jars, has nothing to do with the real thing. Aficionados suggest that half Parmesan and half pecorino cheeses will make the best pesto, others use only one type – some even add ricotta. The pine nuts can be plain or toasted, but ensure that they are fresh, not stale (they turn rancid easily). Make pesto with a mortar and pestle or a food processor, but don't make it too smooth: it should retain some texture and bite.

pesto alla genovese

1 cup pine nuts, lightly pan-toasted

6 garlic cloves, crushed then chopped

1½ cups fresh basil leaves, torn

1 teaspoon coarse salt

⅔ cup freshly grated Parmesan cheese

⅔ cup freshly grated pecorino cheese

⅔ cup extra virgin olive oil

serves 8: makes 1 cup
pasta and gnocchi dishes, with pesto, will serve 4

Grind the pine nuts, garlic, basil, and salt to a paste with a mortar and pestle or in a food processor, using the pulse button.

Keep stirring the paste with one hand (or have the machine still running) while you gradually add half the cheese, then half the olive oil. Repeat the process until you have a rich, stiff, vividly green paste or sauce.

Use within hours if possible (though it keeps, sealed in an airtight container in the refrigerator, for up to 1 week).

Pasta with Pesto (left)

Bring a large saucepan of water to a boil, then add a large pinch of salt. Add 8 small potatoes, halved, and cook for 5 minutes. Add 12 oz. dried trenette or tagliatelle and cook until *al dente*, about 8 minutes more. After about 4 minutes, add 1–2 handfuls of thin green beans. Drain, transfer to a large serving bowl, add about ½ cup of the fresh pesto, toss well, and serve.

Gnocchi with Pesto

Bring a large saucepan of water to a boil, then add a large pinch of salt. Add 1 lb. potato gnocchi and cook until they float to the surface and are chewy textured and well-heated right through. Drain, transfer to a large serving bowl, add about ½ cup of the fresh pesto, toss well, and serve.

Alternatively divide between 4 shallow earthenware dishes, set under a preheated broiler, and cook until bubbling, browned, and aromatic.

In Italy, pasta tends to be served as a *primo piatto*—as a course in itself, after the appetizer or antipasto but before the main dish. Make sure the temperatures are right: the cheese must melt and trickle.

penne with mozzarella and tomatoes

14 oz. penne rigate

14 oz. canned chopped plum tomatoes

1 small dried red chile

3–4 garlic cloves, chopped

1 onion, chopped

2 tablespoons tomato paste

leaves from 2 sprigs of oregano, marjoram, basil, or rosemary, chopped or torn

1 tablespoon sugar

1 tablespoon balsamic vinegar (optional)

2 tablespoons capers, or black olives, rinsed and drained (optional)

sea salt and freshly ground black pepper

to serve

6 oz. mozzarella cheese, sliced thinly, or torn into shreds

2 tablespoons extra virgin olive oil

sprigs of basil

serves 4

Bring a large saucepan of water to a boil, then add a large pinch of salt. Add the penne and cook until *al dente*, about 8 minutes.

Meanwhile, to make the sauce, put the tomatoes in a large, shallow saucepan or skillet. Add the chile, garlic, onion, tomato paste, oregano, sugar, balsamic vinegar, if using, and capers. Cook, stirring, over high heat until the sauce is thick and reduced to half its original volume. Add salt and pepper to taste.

Drain the pasta, reserving 3 tablespoons of the cooking liquid, then return the pasta and reserved liquid to the saucepan. Add the sliced mozzarella. Pour the hot sauce over the top and toss and stir until well mixed and the mozzarella is soft and melting. Sprinkle with the olive oil and serve topped with sprigs of basil.

Variation This dish can also be made in advance. Pour it into a heatproof baking dish, but do not add the cheese. Bake in a preheated oven at 350°F for 25–35 minutes or until very hot, bubbling, and fragrant. Add the cheese and trail the oil on top. Bake for 2 minutes more until the cheese melts, then serve.

A classic, this famous dish was named, some say, after the charcoal burners or coalmen (*carbonari*) from Umbria and Lazio. Other writers, such as Claudia Roden, suggest it may have come about during World War II, with American soldiers bringing their wartime rations of bacon and eggs. Whatever the origins, the bacon and egg are used in a very Italian way. Made well, this dish is delicious and very quick. The cheese, though optional, is frequently included, as is the cream.

spaghetti alla carbonara

14 oz. spaghetti

6 oz. prosciutto or thinly sliced bacon, cut into 1-inch pieces

2 garlic cloves, crushed then chopped

3 extra-large eggs

2 tablespoons thick cream (optional)

1 cup freshly grated Parmesan cheese (optional)

sea salt and freshly ground black pepper

serves 4

Bring a large saucepan of water to a boil, then add a large pinch of salt. Add the spaghetti and cook until *al dente*, about 6–8 minutes.

Put the prosciutto in a heavy skillet and cook until the fat runs and the prosciutto is cooked but barely crisp. Add the garlic. Remove the pan from the heat.

Put the eggs, salt, and pepper in a bowl and beat well, adding the cream, if using. Set aside.

As soon as the spaghetti is ready, drain it and put the bacon pan back over high heat. Toss in the hot pasta, then stir in the eggs and half of the cheese, if using: it sets to a creamy sauce. Remove the pan from the heat. Toss, using tongs, to mix well. Serve with the remaining cheese, if using, on top.

Wide ribbon pasta is particularly popular in Tuscany and also in Umbria. Frequently, it is served with rich meat and game sauces, but freshly made basil oil dressing is a superb alternative. Eat this dish on its own, as a *primo piatto*, or use as an accompaniment.

pappardelle with basil oil

14 oz. dried pappardelle (wide pasta ribbons), plain or frilly edged

⅓ cup extra virgin olive oil

2 garlic cloves, chopped

a handful of fresh chives, chervil, dill, or parsley, plus extra to serve (optional)

2 large handfuls of fresh basil leaves

¼ cup flaked almonds

¼ cup freshly grated pecorino or Parmesan cheese

sea salt and freshly ground black pepper

lemon wedges, to serve (optional)

serves 4

Bring a large saucepan of water to a boil, then add a large pinch of salt. Add the pappardelle and cook until *al dente*, about 8–9 minutes.

Meanwhile, heat half the oil in a skillet, add the garlic, chives, and one handful of the basil leaves. Sauté for 1–1½ minutes or until the greens have wilted and the garlic aromatic.

Transfer to a blender or food processor and blend to a paste. Pour into a plastic or stainless steel (non-reactive) strainer set over a bowl. Press all the oil through with the back of a ladle or wooden spoon.

Heat the remaining olive oil in the skillet, add the almonds, and sauté until golden.

Drain the cooked pasta, add it to the skillet with the almonds, the basil oil, and the remaining basil leaves, the cheese, and extra chives (if using). Add salt and pepper to taste and serve hot or warm, with lemon wedges, if using.

Variation Alternatively, don't strain the basil mixture—just stir it through the cooked pasta and proceed as in the main recipe.

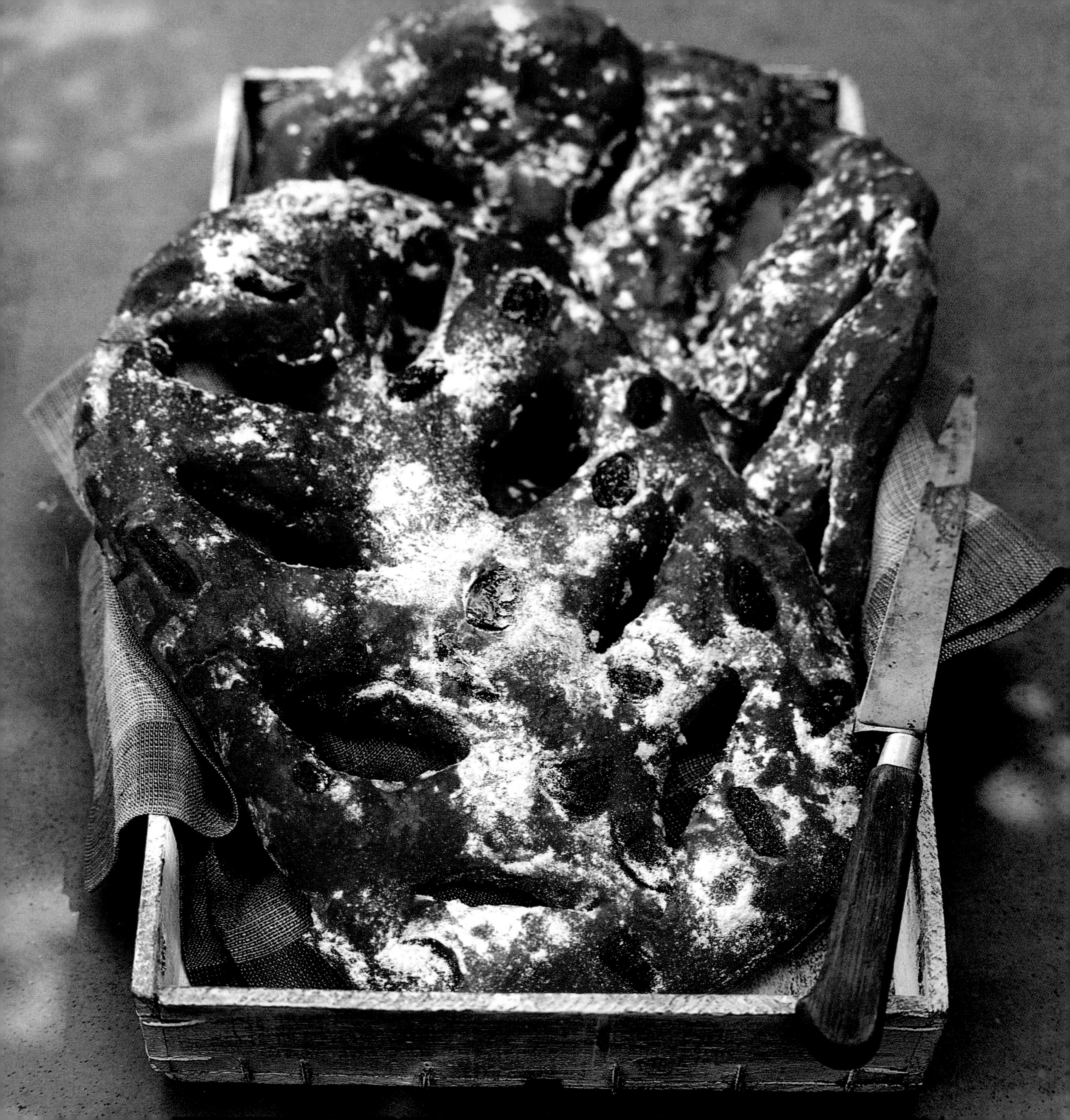

Fougasse belongs to the same ancient family of breads as *focaccie*, the original hearth breads. In Provence, these flat, slashed "ladder breads" (so called because of their shapes) are highly decorative and often flavored with olives or herbs. Sweeter versions contain orange-flower water and almonds and are associated with feast days. Their unusual shape makes them easy to pull apart. Add a little buckwheat, triticale, or spelt flour (see mail order sources, page 142) to the dough and you get even more flavor. Alternatively, use a mixture of white and whole-wheat flours. Good olive oil, delectable olives and herbs create delicious effects.

fougasse

¼ cup extra virgin olive oil, plus extra for baking

2 cups lukewarm water

2 teaspoons honey or syrup (optional)

1⅔ cups whole-wheat flour (or 1⅓ cups malted whole-wheat flour plus ⅓ cup buckwheat, triticale, or spelt flour)

1 teaspoon diastate malt

3⅓ cups bread flour, plus extra for kneading

1 envelope active dry yeast, ¼ oz.

2 teaspoons salt

warm water, for baking

toppings

your choice of:

sliced garlic

onion rings

black olives, cut into strips

unwaxed orange zest, finely sliced

orange-flower water

2 large baking sheets, oiled

makes 4

Put the oil, water, and honey in a measuring cup and stir to dissolve. Put the flour or flours, yeast, and salt in a food processor. With the motor running, pour the liquid through the feed tube to form a dense dough. Stop, then repeat for 30 seconds more, to develop the gluten.

Transfer the dough to a large, oiled bowl, and cover with an oiled plastic bag. Leave in a warm place for at least 30 minutes or up to 2 hours until doubled in volume.

Punch down the risen dough, transfer to a well-floured work surface, and knead for 5–8 minutes or until silky and smooth. Return to the bowl, cover as before, and let rise again for 20 minutes or until doubled in size, then divide into 4. Squeeze, pat, and knead each ball into an oval. Pat or roll out each oval on an oiled baking sheet, until it is 3 times its original size, and about ½ inch thick. Repeat the process with the second fougasse.

Make 2 rows of diagonal slashes in the dough, then open up the slashes to make larger holes. Tug out at the ends and sides if you'd like to open up the dough even more.

Brush the two breads all over with olive oil, then sprinkle with warm water. Add your choice of garlic, onion, olives, orange zest, or orange-flower water.

Bake each fougasse towards the top of a preheated oven at 425°F for 15–20 minutes or until risen, crusty but still chewy. Repeat with the other 2 portions of dough.

Serve warm and eat with your fingers, pulling the bread into short lengths.

Something like a double-thickness, well-stuffed pizza, this ancient recipe is really a kind of substantial double-crust pie. Vary ingredients as you like, though these are fairly typical for a Sicilian recipe—food from this island always seems packed with intense flavors.

schiacciata siciliana

3⅓ cups bread flour, plus extra for shaping

2 tablespoons sugar

1½ teaspoons salt

1 envelope active dry yeast, ¼ oz.

1¼ cups lukewarm water

1 egg, beaten

2 tablespoons extra virgin olive oil

filling

6 oz. caciocavallo or scamorza cheese (smoked mozzarella), chopped or sliced

2 oz. canned anchovies with their oil

4 slices (about 3 oz.) prosciutto or other cured Italian ham, pulled into pieces

2 red or white onions, sliced finely into rings, blanched in boiling water and drained

8 sun-dried tomatoes in oil, chopped

16 green or black olives, pitted

1–1½ teaspoons crumbled dried red chile

1 tablespoon extra virgin olive oil

1 teaspoon sea salt

2 teaspoons cracked black peppercorns

1 teaspoon dried oregano or 2 teaspoons fresh, chopped oregano

a heavy baking sheet, oiled

serves 4–6

Put the flour, sugar, salt, and yeast into a food processor. Pulse a few times to mix and sift.

Put the warm water, egg, and olive oil in a bowl or large measuring cup with a lip and beat well. With the machine running, add the mixture to the processor through the feed tube. The dough will form, clump, then gather in a mass. Remove to a well-floured work surface, sprinkle with extra flour, and knead the dough for 2–3 minutes or until smooth and silky.

Put the ball of dough into a lightly oiled bowl and enclose in a large plastic bag. Leave in a warm place until doubled in size, about 1 hour. Remove from the bowl and punch down the dough. Cut it in half, then roll, pat, and stretch each piece to about 12 inches diameter.

Stretch one of the rounds to about 1 inch more and slide onto a heavy baking tray. Sprinkle it with the cheese, the anchovies and their oil, the proscuitto, onions, tomatoes, olives, and chile. Wet your fingers and sprinkle drops of water all over and around the edges.

Press the remaining round of dough on top. Push down with your knuckles to seal, then use a fork to press and prick all over in a decorative pattern. Press your fingertips all over to make deep indentations. Wet both hands and sprinkle more water on top, then sprinkle with the oil, salt, pepper, and oregano. Let rise in a warm place for about 1 hour or almost doubled in size.

Bake in a preheated oven at 475°F for 15 minutes, then reduce the heat to 400°F and cook for a further 25–30 minutes or until crisp, golden, and fragrant—it should sound hollow when you tap the bottom of the loaf with your knuckles.

Eat hot or warm in squares, segments, or pulled into chunks.

Variation Porcini mushrooms (canned or bottled in oil) can be used instead of olives.

The last time I tasted *coca*, in a fashionable tapas bar in Barcelona, it was cut into uneven chunks and piled hot and high on little plates, then served with olives and glasses of the local wine. It was a revelation. Piquillos are the best peppers to use. If you haven't any, try canned regular peppers, pimientos, or broiled or roasted fresh red bell peppers.

spanish tart with peppers

coca con pimientos

1⅔ cups all-purpose flour

½ envelope active dry yeast, ⅛ oz.

½ teaspoon salt

⅔ cup lukewarm water

topping

¼ cup extra virgin olive oil

2 large red onions, about 12 oz.

about 1 lb. canned sweet red bell peppers, drained

leaves from a small handful of thyme or rosemary sprigs

2 tablespoons anchovy paste, or canned anchovies, chopped and mashed

16 marinated anchovy fillets

a baking sheet, oiled

serves 4–6

To make the dough, put the flour, yeast, and salt in a bowl and mix. Add the water and mix to a satiny dough, then knead, still in the bowl for 5 minutes or until silky. Cover the bowl with a cloth and leave for about 1 hour or until the dough has doubled in size.

Meanwhile, to make the topping, heat 3 tablespoons of the oil in a skillet, add the onions, and cook, stirring over medium heat until softened and transparent. Slice half the peppers and add to the pan. Stir in most of the herbs.

Transfer the dough to a heavy, dark, oiled baking sheet. Punch down, flatten, and roll out the dough to a circle 12 inches diameter. Snip, twist, or roll the edges. Spread all over with the anchovy paste. Add the remaining peppers, left whole, and the cooked onion mixture. Arrange the anchovies and remaining herbs in a decorative pattern on top and sprinkle with the remaining oil.

Bake in a preheated oven at 425°F for 25–30 minutes until the base is crisp and risen, the edges golden, and the filling hot and wilted.

Serve in wedges, hot or cool.

An Italian pizza is really a kind of bread-based open pie, first created from the baker's leftover dough and scraps. Pizza is usually round, sometimes oval, or can be sold in a long rectangle cut into pieces. The glory of a real Neapolitan pizza is its roughness; the wood-fired, uneven, often scorched, and sometimes ashy crust, and the minimal but flavorful toppings bear little relation to the fast-food version. To make pizza at home, it helps to have a pizza stone or flat earthenware tile to bake it on. If not, use a heavy, old, dark, metal baking sheet, which will hold the heat well.

pizza napoletana

3⅓ cups bread flour, plus extra for shaping
2 tablespoons sugar
1½ teaspoons salt
1 envelope active dry yeast, ¼ oz.
1⅓ cups lukewarm water
1 egg, beaten
2 tablespoons extra virgin olive oil

topping

14 oz. canned chopped plum tomatoes
2 garlic cloves, chopped
1 tablespoon sugar
¼ cup extra virgin olive oil
a large handful of fresh basil leaves, torn
24 anchovies
24 capers
1 dried red chile, crumbled (optional)
8 oz. mozzarella cheese, sliced (optional)
24 black olives, pitted

1 pizza stone or baking sheet
a pizza peel

makes 4

Put the flour, sugar, salt, and yeast into a food processor. Pulse a few times to mix and sift.

Put the warm water, egg, and olive oil in a bowl or large measuring cup with a lip and beat well. With the machine running, add the mixture to the processor through the feed tube. The dough will form, clump, then gather in a mass. Remove to a well-floured work surface, sprinkle with extra flour, and knead the dough for 2–3 minutes or until smooth and silky.

Put the ball of dough into a lightly oiled bowl and enclose in a large plastic bag. Leave in a warm place until doubled in size, about 1 hour. Remove the dough from the bowl and punch it down. Cut it into 4 pieces. Meanwhile, preheat the pizza stone or baking sheet on the top oven shelf at 425°F until very hot.

Put the pieces of dough on a well-floured surface and shape into rounds about ½ inch thick, but thicker around the edges. Make indentations with your fingertips. Let rise again while you make the topping.

Meanwhile, put the canned tomatoes in a large, shallow saucepan, then add the garlic, sugar, 2 tablespoons of the oil, and half the basil leaves. Bring to a boil and cook, uncovered, for 8–12 minutes until reduced by half. When ready to cook, use a peel to slide 1 pizza dough base onto the hot pizza stone. Spread hot tomato sauce on top leaving about 1 inch bare at the edges. Sprinkle with the anchovies, capers, and chile, if using.

Bake in a preheated oven at 425°F for about 10–12 minutes or until risen, blistered, hot, and fragrant. Add the remaining basil and trickle the remaining oil over the top. Serve the first pizza and repeat to make the remaining 3. Eat hot or warm, using fingers to fold up each quarter.

sweet things

Around the Mediterranean, sweet things appear at any time of day, though often not as dessert at the end of a meal. Sticky cakes, pastries, and cookies are often eaten with a milky coffee at breakfast, or with espresso later as a restorative. Ice cream is licked from cones while strolling the streets at the end of the day—the *passeggiata*. Whole families sit down to extravagant assemblages of gelati or sorbetti, decorated with multicolored candies and wafer cookies sailing like spinnakers on top.

Such delicious treats are very often not produced at home, but bought from speciality shops, the *patisserie*, the *gelateria*, the *panaderia*.

Many were created, originally, to celebrate festivals, Saints' days or holidays. Sweet things add color and excitement to the day, celebrate the seasons, and offer an easy way to be hospitable. A few Greek pastries, a glass of ice water, a tiny frothy black coffee—all create a refreshing snack, at any time of the day. Add a *digestivo* of fruit brandy, liqueur, Marsala, or some famed Pedro Ximenez aged sherry, and you'll feel like a million euros.

Honey from Provence is superbly floral, especially the unblended, single-flower varieties. Lavender, mimosa, and some wildflower honeys are often outstandingly intense, but clear and pale. In contrast, some Greek mountain honeys (such as *hymettus*) are often dark with extreme, rich complexity. This elegant end to a meal is essentially French, but it also could work well using Greek-style honey and a soft young feta cheese made with goat or sheep milk. Ripe, sticky figs, which often grow wild along the roadsides, are one of the joys of the Mediterranean, whether they are white figs (actually pale green) or black (actually velvety purple). This is simple but perfect.

provençal goat cheese
with lavender honey

about 8 oz. young fresh goat cheeses, such as chèvre, chabichou, or crottin de chavignol, or a mixture

4 ripe figs

¼ cup scented, single-flower honey, such as Provençal lavender honey

praline (optional)

¼ cup sugar

½ cup pine nuts or shelled blanched pistachios

to serve

lavender blossoms (optional)

crisp wafer cookies

a metal tray

serves 4

If making the praline, mix the sugar and nuts in a clean, dry skillet over high heat. Move and shake the pan from side to side over the heat, never stirring, until the base sugar, and then the top layer, begins to melt. When the color changes from medium gold to deep gold, reduce the heat. Cook for 15–30 seconds longer (1–4 minutes altogether), then pour the caramelized nuts out onto a metal tray. Let cool and set.

Arrange the cheeses on 4 small plates.

Cut the figs in half, or split them in 4 from the tops, and pull open into flower shapes. Break the praline, if using, into large shards and crush some of the fragments. Sprinkle the praline over the cheeses, then trickle honey over the top. Add a few lavender blossoms, if using, to reinforce the scent, and serve with crisp cookies.

These superb caramelized egg custards scented with strips of lemon zest are one of the joys of Spain. This version is from Catalonia. Often they are made in small, shallow, individual, earthenware dishes, glazed on the inside. Catalonia once briefly included Sicily, Sardinia, and Naples, so there are interesting culinary influences from these neighboring cuisines. Spanish cooks may caramelize the sugar on top using an old-fashioned salamander, a traditional metal implement, heated over coal or a hot element. One alternative is a preheated grill, while today's chefs and cooks use a blowtorch instead. Be sure to have the heat source very hot—you do not want to damage, melt, or toughen the delicate custard beneath by undue browning. This version is lighter than the French variety, *crème caramel*, and tastes wonderful.

spanish flans
crema quemada

⅔ cup light cream and milk, mixed half and half

zest of 1 unwaxed lemon, cut into 8 long strips, bruised

¼ cup sugar

3 eggs, preferably free-range

2 teaspoons pure vanilla extract

¼ cup sugar, to glaze

4 shallow heatproof dishes, ⅓ cup each

a baking pan

a cook's blowtorch (optional)

serves 4

Put the cream, milk, and 4 of the strips of lemon zest in a saucepan and heat almost to boiling (this is called scalding). Put the pan in a bowl of ice water to cool it quickly. Put the sugar, eggs, and vanilla in a bowl and beat until well blended, trying to avoid making froth. Stir in the cooled scalded cream.

Pour the custard mixture into the 4 dishes. Add the remaining strips of lemon zest: tuck one into each custard.

Set the dishes in a baking pan and add enough boiling water to come halfway up the sides of the dishes. Bake towards the top of a preheated oven at 325°F for 20 minutes or until very gently set and wobbly. Remove the baking pan from the oven, then remove the dishes from the pan.

Sprinkle the sugar evenly over each custard. Preheat an overhead broiler to very hot, leaving space for the pots to be 1 inch from the heat. Alternatively turn on the blowtorch. Broil or blowtorch the custards until a fine layer of caramel forms on top. Serve, preferably at room temperature, within 2 hours.

In English, *panna cotta* simply means "cooked cream," and essentially that is what it is, with some additional flavorings and setting agents (these can vary greatly). With hints of vanilla, almond, and rose, this is a luxurious version. Scented syrup and rose petals are the final touch for a captivating taste of the sunny Mediterranean.

panna cotta
with rose-petal syrup

1 tablespoon gelatin granules

⅔ cup light cream

1 vanilla bean, split lengthwise, seeds removed with the point of a knife

⅓ cup sugar

1 lb. mascarpone cheese

½ teaspoon pure almond extract or 1 tablespoon Amaretto liqueur

1 teaspoon rose water

syrup

2 tablespoons vanilla sugar

½ cup white wine

to serve

1 scented rose, pulled into petals

6–8 cantucci or amaretti cookies (optional)

6–8 small pots, cups, or dishes, ½ cup each, oiled

serves 6–8

Put the gelatin in a heatproof bowl, add ¼ cup water, and leave to swell.

Put the cream, vanilla bean, and its seeds in a small saucepan, heat to simmering, then almost to boiling, then turn off the heat. Let stand for 2 minutes.

Stir in the soaked gelatin until it dissolves. Remove the vanilla bean (you can dry it and use it to perfume a jar of sugar).

Put the sugar, mascarpone, almond extract, and ½ teaspoon of the rose water in a bowl and beat until creamy and smooth. Whisk in the gelatin mixture. Pour into the prepared pots, cups, or dishes and chill for at least 2 hours.

Meanwhile, to make the syrup, put the vanilla sugar and white wine in a small saucepan over gentle heat and stir until dissolved and bubbling. Let cool slightly, then stir in the remaining rose water.

Serve the panna cotta in their pots, or turned out, with a trickle of syrup and several scented rose petals, and crisp cookies such as cantucci or amaretti.

All over France, the fruits of gnarled old orchard trees are used for cooking, in preserves, and to make wines, ratafias, and fruit cordials. In early times, in country areas, a traveling still would make its rounds once a year and distil some of the fruit wine into eau-de-vie, a kind of schnapps, often very powerful. These days, fruit brandies are relatively easy to find at quality liquor stores. Such flavors give real intensity to the syrup, which can also be useful in many different situations, for instance with fresh berries, over cakes, and with ice cream.

château peaches

4 perfectly ripe fresh peaches, preferably free-stone type

1 cup water or unsweetened peach juice

¼ cup vanilla sugar or sugar

¼ cup eau-de-vie, such as apricot, peach, pear, plum, or raspberry

1½ cups (about 8 oz.) ripe raspberries

8 ladyfinger cookies, to serve

4 large brandy snifters, wineglasses, glass bowls, or fine china dishes

serves 4

Using a small knife, cut a small cross into the base and stalk ends of each peach.

Put the water or juice and sugar in a medium saucepan and bring to a boil. Stir until the sugar has dissolved, then reduce to simmering. Add the peaches and splash and spoon the hot syrup all over them. Leave for 3–5 minutes—in this time, they will cook very delicately and the skins will loosen. Try to avoid bruising the flesh.

Use a slotted spoon to remove the peaches onto a plate. Pull off and discard the skins. Cool the syrup.

To serve, put 1 peach into each glass or bowl. Stir the eau-de-vie into the cooled syrup, then spoon it over the peaches and add raspberries. Serve with cookies.

Variations

• Nectarines or plums, though less delicate, could be substituted if no ripe peaches are available, but you won't have to peel them.

• For an unusual cocktail, mix the pink syrup from this recipe with ice and extra eau-de-vie.

Strawberries, when freshly picked and at the height of their summery sweetness, are a joy: they should be simply eaten on their own. At other times strawberries may need a little assistance to coax out their full potential, as in this recipe. The interesting mix of flavors is an echo of the medieval, and often medicinal, use of spices and balsams.

sugared strawberries
fragole con ricotta medievale

2 pints ripe, red strawberries, washed, dried, hulled, and halved

8 oz. fresh ricotta cheese, 1 cup

1 tablespoon Amaretto liqueur, plus extra to serve

½ teaspoon balsamic vinegar

spiced sugar

½ stick of cinnamon, crushed

6 peppercorns, crushed

⅓ cup sugar

3-inch strip of unwaxed lemon zest

serves 4

To make the spiced sugar, put the cinnamon, peppercorns, sugar, and zest in an electric coffee grinder or small spice grinder. Grind in continuous bursts to make a powdery spiced mixture.

Put the strawberries in a bowl and spoon half the mixture on top, gently stirring and mixing to encourage the juices to run. Leave for 10 minutes. Meanwhile, press the ricotta through a strainer into a bowl with the back of a spoon. Mix in the liqueur, the remaining spiced sugar, and the vinegar to form a cream.

To serve, put spoonfuls of the creamy mixture in small, stemmed glasses or glass or china dishes, then pile the berries on top and sprinkle them with a few extra drops of liqueur.

In this version of the famous Venetian dessert, a sort of Italian trifle cake, layers of cookies have an alcohol-boosted creamy filling, and coffee and chocolate as flavorings. Although this dessert can be eaten fresh, it can also be partially or fully frozen and eaten when near to room temperature again. It is worth investing in some authentic Italian Marsala: it distinguishes this dish and is an invaluable kitchen ingredient. The almond-flavored liqueur, Amaretto di Saronno, is another useful pantry item, for elegant quick drinks and desserts.

semifreddo al tiramisù

¼ cup dry Marsala

7 egg yolks

⅓ cup vanilla sugar

1 cup mascarpone cheese or cream cheese, about 8 oz.

⅔ cup heavy cream, whipped and chilled

½ cup espresso coffee or strong, freshly made coffee

¼ cup Amaretto liqueur

24 savoiardi cookies (ladyfingers)

2 tablespoons unsweetened cocoa powder

2 tablespoons confectioners' sugar

¼ cup extra Marsala or Amaretto, for serving

a large loaf pan, 9 x 5 x 3 inches, lined with a double layer of aluminum foil, ends hanging out and overlapping the long sides

serves 4

Put the Marsala in a heatproof bowl set over a saucepan of boiling water. Heat until very hot, then remove from the heat.

Put the egg yolks and sugar in a second bowl over the saucepan of boiling water, beat until pale and frothy, then beat in the hot Marsala.

Cool the frothy mixture over a bowl of ice water, still beating constantly. Gradually beat in the mascarpone. Fold in the cream. Set aside.

Put the coffee and liqueur in a shallow bowl and mix well. Dip 8 cookies, sugared side up, into the coffee-liqueur mix. Layer them in the base of the prepared loaf pan, sugared side down. Smooth in half of the creamy cheese mixture. Add a second layer of dipped cookies, then add a second layer of creamy cheese mixture. Put the final 8 dipped cookies on top with the sugared sides up.

Sift the cocoa and sugar together, then use to dust the top of the dessert. Fold the foil over the top to enclose. Freeze for 3–4 hours or until semi-frozen. Unfold and serve in slices, semi-frozen, with another dusting of cocoa mixture, and pour a little Marsala or Amaretto around each serving.

Gelato must be one of Italy's most loved and appreciated exports, and Italian ice cream makers all over the world have delighted their local communities wherever they set up shop. In Naples recently, I was enthralled by the astounding rainbow array of ices in every gelateria: nut ices of great complexity, chocolate, coffee, and caramel flavors from bitter to mellow, and berry ices of wonderful intensity. This version uses apricot and orange. For a change, serve it between crisp wafers, cookies, or even slices of brioche, a traditional idea.

apricot and orange gelato

8 oz. dried apricots, 1¼ cups, chopped

¾ cup plus 2 tablespoons sugar

2 teaspoons freshly grated orange zest and 1 cup freshly squeezed orange juice, about 2–3 unwaxed oranges

3 tablespoons freshly squeezed lemon juice, about 1 medium lemon

1 teaspoon orange-flower water

2 tablespoon Cointreau (or other citrus liqueur)

8 oz. mascarpone cheese, in pieces

1¾ cups light cream

8–12 wafers, cookies, sliced brioche or lemon cakes (optional)

an electric ice cream maker

6-cup freezerproof container with a lid

serves 4–6

Put the chopped apricots in a saucepan and cover with boiling water by about 1 inch. Return to a boil, reduce the heat, and simmer for 10 minutes. Turn off the heat. Let stand for 5 minutes.

Put the apricots and their cooking water in a blender (for smooth texture) or food processor (for coarse texture), then add the sugar, orange zest, orange and lemon juices, orange-flower water, and liqueur. Blend well. Add the mascarpone pieces. Blend briefly until the mixture is even and smooth. Pour out half and set aside.

Add the cream to the machine. Blend very briefly again until incorporated, then pour both mixtures into a large bowl, stirring well. Cool, if necessary, over ice water.

Transfer the mixture to an ice cream maker and churn for 20–35 minutes or until thick. Spoon into the freezerproof container, cover, and freeze until time to use. Alternatively, freeze in the container, covered, for 6 hours, beating it once, after 3 hours. Serve in scoops or slices with cookies or cake, if using.

Note When sharply flavored fresh apricots are in season, halve, pit, and broil or bake 1 lb. (8–12 fruit) until they are collapsed, golden, and tender. Use these in place of the dried apricots: they need no further cooking.

Italian and French gelaterias offer splendid, often simple flavor combinations. Chocolate and nuts are particularly delicious, especially if the chocolate is of the high-quality, bittersweet type. If you have a mortar and pestle, try to pound the nuts and sugar to a very smooth texture—otherwise use an electric coffee grinder or spice grinder in short bursts.

bitter chocolate and hazelnut gelato

½ cup blanched (peeled) hazelnuts, finely chopped

1 cup vanilla sugar or sugar

⅔ cup whole milk

8 oz. bittersweet chocolate, broken in pieces

1 tablespoon corn syrup

1 tablespoon chocolate or hazelnut liqueur or dark rum

1¾ cups heavy cream

crisp wafers or cookies, to serve (optional)

an electric ice cream maker
or a 1-quart freezerproof container

serves 4–6

Put the chopped hazelnuts in a dry skillet and dry-cook over moderate heat, stirring constantly until they darken and smell toasty, about 2–3 minutes (take care, because they burn easily). Pour out onto a plate and let cool.

Put the toasted hazelnuts and ¼ cup of the sugar in a small electric spice grinder or coffee grinder. Grind in brief bursts, to a smooth, speckly powder.

Put the milk, chocolate, and remaining sugar in a saucepan over very gentle heat. Cook until the chocolate melts, stirring constantly, then add the corn syrup and ground sugar and nuts. Remove from the heat, put the pan into a bowl of ice water and let cool. Stir in the liqueur and cream and cool again.

Pour the prepared mixture into the ice cream maker and churn for 20–25 minutes or until set. Alternatively, freeze in the container, covered, for 6 hours, beating it once, after 3 hours.

Serve in scoops with wafers or cookies, if using.

Lemon tart—wobbly, sharp, creamy, but acidic—is an outrageously delicious dish. In France, these are often slim, very elegant offerings, not heavily filled. The ideal is to make it a few hours before you intend to eat it, then serve it warm or cool. Some ice-cold scoops of thick sharp crème fraîche or whipped cream are the perfect accompaniment. Serve with a small glass of citrus liqueur, dark rum, or brandy.

french lemon tart
tarte aux citrons

6 tablespoons confectioners' sugar, sifted

1½ sticks butter, at room temperature

2 egg yolks

2 tablespoons ice water

1⅔ cups all-purpose flour, sifted

lemon filling

4 eggs

¾ cup superfine sugar

2 tablespoons shredded lemon zest, from 2–3 unwaxed lemons

½ cup heavy cream, plus extra to serve

a shallow false-bottom 8-inch tart pan, no more than 1 inch deep, set on a baking sheet

wax paper and baking beans

serves 4

To make the dough, set aside 2 tablespoons of the confectioners' sugar and put the remainder in the bowl of an electric mixer. Add the butter and beat until creamy, soft, and white. Add the egg yolks one at a time and continue beating until well mixed. Trickle in half the ice water, then add the flour. Beat on a lower speed, adding the remaining water until the dough gathers into a soft ball. Wrap in plastic wrap, and chill for 40–60 minutes.

Transfer the dough to a floured work surface and roll out to ¼ inch thick. Use it to line the tart pan. Gently push the dough into the corners. Cut off the excess dough. Chill for a further 20 minutes or until very firm.

Prick the dough all over with a fork, line with wax paper, fill with baking beans, and bake blind in a preheated oven at 350°F for 15 minutes. Remove the paper and the beans. Let the pastry rest for 5 minutes, then bake again for 10 minutes or until pale golden.

To make the filling, put the eggs, sugar, and half the lemon zest in a bowl and beat well for 2 minutes with a hand-held electric mixer. Stir in the lemon juice and crème fraîche, then pour the mixture into the tart crust. Bake at 250°F for 35 minutes, or until the filling is barely set.

While the tart cooks, put the remaining lemon zest in a sieve, pour over boiling water, then refresh under cold running water. Put the zest, the reserved 2 tablespoons confectioners' sugar. and ¼ cup water in a saucepan over low heat. Cook gently until the zest looks syrupy. Sprinkle the zest over the cooked tart. Serve hot or warm, with additional spoonfuls of heavy cream.

Variation Dust with additional confectioners' sugar and serve with a scoop of vanilla ice cream.

greek custard pie
galaktoboureko

filling

1 quart milk

1 cup plus 2 tablespoons fine semolina

4 extra-large eggs, beaten lightly

1 cup sugar

1 teaspoon pure vanilla extract

dough

2 sticks butter, melted, warm

8 oz. phyllo pastry dough or 16 sheets

syrup

½ cup flower-scented honey

¾ cup vanilla sugar

⅓ cup fresh orange juice

2 teaspoons finely grated orange zest

1 teaspoon orange-flower water

fruit

2 large ripe peaches or nectarines,
cut into 8 segments each

24 pistachios, blanched and peeled

½ cup sugar

a round or square metal baking pan, about 10 inches square or 12 inches diameter

serves 8

To make the filling, put the milk and semolina in a saucepan, and heat gently, stirring frequently, then bring to a boil for 1 minute. Reduce the heat and simmer for a further 6 minutes.

Put the eggs in a bowl with the sugar and vanilla and beat until frothy. Still stirring, pour some of the hot milk mixture into the eggs to warm them, then pour the mixture back in the saucepan and cook, stirring constantly over low heat, for 2–3 minutes, or until the custard is creamy and comes away from the sides of the saucepan. Put the saucepan in a bowl of ice water to cool it quickly, stirring now and then to prevent a skin forming.

To make the dough, brush the baking pan inside with the melted butter. Lay 1 sheet of phyllo across the pan, letting extra hang over the sides. Brush all over with melted butter. Repeat the process in the opposite direction. Repeat 4 times more in alternate directions, brushing each phyllo sheet with butter before positioning it, and keeping the unused phyllo covered with plastic and a cloth.

Add the cool custard, smoothing the top. Leaving the phyllo overhanging the edges, use the remaining phyllo sheets to cover the custard, brushing with the butter as before. Do not butter the last sheet of phyllo. Push the phyllo sheets down between the edge of the custard and the outer phyllo sheets, like tucking in bed sheets. Scrunch up the outer overhangs of phyllo and gather them up to make a decorative edge.

Using a short, very sharp serrated knife or a razor blade, make a series of parallel cuts into the phyllo in one direction, then at an oblique angle in the opposite direction at 1-inch intervals to make a diamond pattern. Brush any remaining butter over the top.

Bake in a preheated oven at 350°F for 50 minutes. The dough should be deep gold and the custard wobbly, but just firm.

To make the syrup, put the honey, sugar, orange juice, and ⅔ cup water in a saucepan and cook for 6 minutes until dissolved. Cool slightly, then add the zest.

Remove the pie from the oven. Cut the surface again, using the same score marks, through the custard to its base. Stir the orange-flower water into the syrup, then pour over the pie until it is well soaked. Arrange the fruit segments over the top of the pie and sprinkle with the pistachios.

Put the sugar in a dry skillet. Heat, shaking the pan from side to side but never stirring, until the sugar melts, darkens, and caramelizes, about 4–5 minutes. Carefully pour it, sizzling, all over the fruit-covered pie in a series of lines. Let stand for 5 minutes to set the caramel and cool it slightly. Cut in wedges or diamond-shaped chunks and serve warm or cool, not hot.

Fragrant, crumbly *kourambiedes* in fancy boxes are sold in grocers' shops or freshly made from a patisserie or *galaktoplasteion*, but the best are homemade. They are served all year round, but especially at Christmas, usually with syrupy fruit and nut preserves, known as *glyka* or "spoon sweets."

greek shortbread cookies
kourambiedes

1 stick plus 6 tablespoons butter, at room temperature

½ cup plus 1 tablespoon sugar

2 egg yolks

1 teaspoon vanilla extract

2 tablespoons Greek Metaxa brandy or Cognac

20 green cardamom pods, crushed, black seeds extracted or 1 stick cinnamon, ground to a powder

½ cup flaked almonds, chopped or crushed

1 teaspoon baking powder, sifted

2⅔ cups all-purpose flour, sifted

to serve

2 tablespoons rose water

2 tablespoons Greek Metaxa brandy or Cognac

1½ cups sifted confectioners' sugar

2 baking sheets, greased with 2 tablespoons butter

wax paper

makes about 32

Put the butter and sugar in a bowl and beat until light and pale. Beat in the egg yolks, vanilla, brandy, cardamom, and almonds. Add the baking powder and about two-thirds of the flour and stir to form a soft, sticky dough. Stir in enough of the remaining flour to make a soft, manageable dough.

Take 1 heaping tablespoon of dough, put it on a floured work surface, and roll it into an oval. Set it on one of the prepared baking sheets, then push and pinch the ends into a half-moon shape. Pinch up the middle of the crescent so it is high and deeply curved. Repeat with the remaining dough to make about 32–34, shared between the trays.

Bake in a preheated oven at 325°F for 16–18 minutes or until pale, golden, firm, crisp, and crumbly, then remove and let cool on wire racks.

Mix the rose water and brandy in a small bowl or cup. Put the confectioners' sugar in another. Brush, sprinkle, or partially dip each cookie quickly with some of the flavoring, then dip each quickly into the sifted confectioners' sugar until very thickly coated. Lift out and store in a container lined with wax paper, in layers if necessary.

Note *Kourambiedes* served with a glass of Greek brandy and a tiny cup of Greek coffee—*sketo* (unsweetened), *metrio* (medium-sweet), or *glyka* (very sweet)—make a truly charming late-afternoon offering (when dinner is likely to be late) or after a meal instead of dessert.

mail order and websites

Gourmet shops and quality supermarkets are generally well-stocked with the Italian or French ingredients you might need for forays into Mediterranean cooking. Authentic Spanish ingredients are just beginning to make their way onto American shelves.

Tienda.com
757-566-8606 or 888-472-1022
3701 Rochambeau Road
Williamsburg, VA 23188

This well-organized, easy-to-navigate website offers a treasure of Spanish specialty food products including Cabrales cheese, Calasparra rice for paella, sweet, bittersweet or hot smoked paprika, pequillo peppers, aged sherry vinegars and olive oil. Meats include jamón serrano (sliced or an entire ham) and many chorizos. Sign up for a catalog.

www.zingermans.com
620 Phoenix Drive
Ann Arbor, Michigan 48108
888-636-8162 or 734-663-DELI
422 Detroit Street
Ann Arbor, Michigan 48104

What began in 1982 as small deli with great sandwiches has grown to a global foods paradise. Zingerman's selection of cheeses, estate-bottled olive oils and varietal vinegars is unmatched. Their website and catalog are packed with information.

www.chefshop.com
877-337-2491
P.O. Box 3488
Seattle, WA 98114

Features a wide range of quality raw ingredients, plus condiments and seasonings. The selection of American and European floral honeys is particularly enticing.

www.turkishtaste.com
603-661-5460
P.O. Box 825
Greenland NH 03840

Running low on pomegranate molasses or any number of Turkish delights? Browse the on-line shelves of Turkish Taste.

www.penzeys.com
800-741-7787

Penzeys Spice offers more than 250 herbs, spices and seasonings, including blue poppyseeds, white, green, or pink peppercorns, white and green cardamom, and premium saffron. Shop on-line, request a catalog or explore any one of 16 Penzeys Spice shops nationwide.

www.kingarthurflour.com
800-827-6836
P.O. Box 876
Norwich, VT 05055

King Arthur Flour, Vermont's venerable milling company, has on-line site and catalogue called "The Bakers Catalogue" that is an invaluable resource for serious (and not-so-serious) bread bakers. You may order every flour imaginable including spelt, buckwheat, triticale flours, plus malt products and other baking aids. Knowledgeable staff is available to answer baking questions: call 802-649-3717.

www.greekproducts.com
Pindou 21, 22 Argyroupolis
16451 Athens, Greece
Tel: +30 210 994 9770/3231
Fax: +30 210 994 9771

About Greek food and Greek food producers.

www.greekshops.com
GreekShops.com
6 Skiathou St, Suite Vesta
11254 Athens, Greece
Tel: +30 (01) 2219-910
Fax: +30 (01) 2289-945

Delivers quality and/or hard-to-find Greek products around the world.

index

conversion charts

Weights and measures have been rounded up or down slightly to make measuring easier.

Volume equivalents:

American	*Metric*	*Imperial*
1 teaspoon	5 ml	
1 tablespoon	15 ml	
¼ cup	60 ml	2 fl.oz.
⅓ cup	75 ml	2½ fl.oz.
½ cup	125 ml	4 fl.oz.
⅔ cup	150 ml	5 fl.oz. (¼ pint)
¾ cup	175 ml	6 fl.oz.
1 cup	250 ml	8 fl.oz.

Weight equivalents:

Imperial	*Metric*
1 oz.	25 g
2 oz.	50 g
3 oz.	75 g
4 oz.	125 g
5 oz.	150 g
6 oz.	175 g
7 oz.	200 g
8 oz. (½ lb.)	250 g
9 oz.	275 g
10 oz.	300 g
11 oz.	325 g
12 oz.	375 g
13 oz.	400 g
14 oz.	425 g
15 oz.	475 g
16 oz. (1 lb.)	500 g
2 lb.	1 kg

Measurements:

Inches	*Cm*
¼ inch	5 mm
½ inch	1 cm
¾ inch	1.5 cm
1 inch	2.5 cm
2 inches	5 cm
3 inches	7 cm
4 inches	10 cm
5 inches	12 cm
6 inches	15 cm
7 inches	18 cm
8 inches	20 cm
9 inches	23 cm
10 inches	25 cm
11 inches	28 cm
12 inches	30 cm

Oven temperatures:

110°C	(225°F)	Gas ¼
120°C	(250°F)	Gas ½
140°C	(275°F)	Gas 1
150°C	(300°F)	Gas 2
160°C	(325°F)	Gas 3
180°C	(350°F)	Gas 4
190°C	(375°F)	Gas 5
200°C	(400°F)	Gas 6
220°C	(425°F)	Gas 7
230°C	(450°F)	Gas 8
240°C	(475°F)	Gas 9